The camper's handbook

The camper's handbook

A complete guide to wilderness and family camping in North America

by
John Power

Illustrated by E. B. Sanders

MODERN CANADIAN LIBRARY
TORONTO

A — 4.73 (I)

Printed and bound in Canada
Library of Congress Catalog Card Number 72-12169
SBN 684-13333-4

CONTENTS

To Michael, Susan, Sandra and Sean, with the hope that our great outdoors with all its pleasures and freedoms will endure for you and your children.

And to my good friend, Frank Wice, who shares most of my philosophies and has shared many of my outdoor experiences.

INTRODUCTION

Whether you camp as part of the hunting, fishing or photography package; or because it affords a glimpse at a vanishing heritage; or for its therapeutic value as a respite from our galloping lifestyle; or just because it is the only way the entire family can afford a vacation together; whatever your motivations are; this book was written with you in mind.

Campers obviously seek more than the experience of a night under canvas. That you can have by pitching a tent in your back yard.

Perhaps the current exodus to the outdoors is a reflection of our somewhat recent appreciation of nature, a change in priorities.

Abundance doesn't breed appreciation. Only when something becomes scarce or is being taken from us do we place a high value on it.

In these pages I have passed on hints, tips, ideas and philosophies which have accumulated over three decades of frequent pitches.

The outdoors is a friend, not a foe. It is a place to enjoy yourself and enjoy its bounty. It is where acquantances become friends; friends become closer; families become more tightly knit; and where you even get to know yourself better.

Whatever your faith, you can reflect and/or meditate in a log chapel, where the logs are vertical and still have branches attached.

This is not only a how-to book, it is a how-not-to,

based on my own foibles. You can profit from my mistakes just as I have. Those who have traveled the same crooked path know whereof I speak.

Equipment, techniques, wilderness know-how, creatures of the forests, first aid and countless other facets of camping are discussed in depth, but in a light-hearted style.

This is not a text book. I've never been able to keep my nose in one, and have no intention of ever writing such a book. While there is so much to learn in the great outdoors that few are ever grade A students, it is not a scholarly subject.

Camping and outdoor living are fascinating, and they are fun. You're bound to fumble and bumble until you get to know the ropes. Don't worry. You will soon become competent as you listen, look, and learn. Above all, have a good time.

Outdoor life fosters tolerance, independence and a sense of humour. If the outdoors weren't like a foreign country to those legions who have no kinship with it, the world would have fewer problems. The anecdotes, reflections and experiences with which this book is liberally sprinkled all contain a message.

This is a complete guide to camping, which I hope you will enjoy reading as much as I have enjoyed writing it.

Chapter One

GEAR

TENTS AND TARPS

The tent one buys is a matter of choice. But, because the range is so vast, it is easy for the newly-indoctrinated camper to select the wrong one.

Neophytes are confused by a seemingly endless array of sizes, shapes, styles, prices and colors. Which is best? Why? Finally, they become so confused that they would like to forget about the whole business.

Before getting into a flap, boil your choice down to your needs and budget.

Your requirements will differ if you are looking for a tent suitable for family camping in a campground, or a tent for backpacking.

Weight is of little concern if you are driving to within pitching distance of your campsite. But if you intend to tote it for miles on your shoulders, then light weight is a requisite.

Bulk is not too important when the tent goes from car trunk to site in a few easy steps, but if it has to be squeezed into a pack, it becomes a different story.

Style is dictated by weather, winds, exposure and

personal preference. Size is determined by the number of bodies who will be bedding down in it, and the length of stay. Price is a personal problem, and color depends on individual taste.

Years ago, when most tents were green, white or brown, I owned a bright orange one. Sun and rain took their toll over a period of time, and it faded to beige. But that tent was a spirit-lifting shelter, both inside and out. Nowadays, there is no dearth of gay and gaudy tent fabrics.

Put a little color in your camp-life. To heck with highfalutin talk about blending your tent with the landscape. A bright canvas against a green woodland setting is a pretty sight.

I personally prefer a largish tent, because I like to stand up to dress; and, if tent-bound by really inclement weather, I do not feel cooped-up.

If you make your pitch in a campground, consider buying the "umbrella"—sometimes called "tourist"—the "cottage", or the "igloo". Also, don't count out the old fashioned wall tent.

Umbrella tents have been long-time favourites and rightly so. Most of these tents measure an ample nine feet by nine feet, and some even go to nine feet by twelve feet. They have sufficient headroom to allow the occupants to stand up, an awning over the zippered door, and at least one inside window. The economy models are supported by a center pole instead of outside rods. But outside rods are well worth the extra few dollars, as they keep your shelter taut and do not encroach on that precious inside space.

Cottage tents can rival a cabin in area. An average model boasts about 180 square feet, and some are even larger. Most have a second room, thus permitting an entire family to sleep under one roof. It takes a while to erect a shelter of these dimensions, so it is not recommended for campers on the move.

The igloo comes in various sizes; seven foot and nine foot diameters are the most popular.

The smaller igloo is a good bet for canoe trips, if long portages are not planned, as the smaller igloo is inclined to be rather bulky and heavy. It is also slightly skimpy on space, and cannot rival the roominess afforded by those few extra square feet of the larger model. The nine-footer provides plenty of headroom. Both come with fiberglass outside rods and can be erected quickly and easily. A similar style is one braced by inflatable struts. Inside weight will hold the struts in place, so pegging is not necessary.

The wall tent needs no description. This is the traditional model used by campers since the year one, and still favored by many bushmen and outfitters. Wall tents are commodious, they can be rigged with poles from the forest, and stovepipes can be installed in permanent camps.

Other models are legion, from "add a room" tents ideal for families, to the larger wing types which are excellent for windy pitches by sea or lakeshore.

People who prefer canoe tripping or a more private setting than found in populated campgrounds, must usually sacrifice space in the interests of lightness and compactness.

One exception is the lean-to-shaped Baker tent, which can sleep three. The front wall extends into a canopy, under which a tall man can walk without taking off his hat.

In lightweight Egyptian cotton, this tent weighs as little as ten pounds.

Even ten pounds is too much for backpackers, who will want to cut that load in half, or even less.

Is a sewn-in floor in a tent a good idea? For many years I said "no", with good reason. It was, almost without exception, made of heavy duck material which added pounds of weight and was impossible to keep clean. Once the dirt of a few trips was ground in, the shelter looked a mess. Furthermore, mildew problems arose if you were pitched in one place for long.

This type of poor flooring is still found in the lower-priced tents, but nowadays most of the better models have a coated-nylon floor which is damp-proof, and may be wiped clean.

Unless your jaunts are confined to the bug-free altitudes of mountain slopes, your tent should be outfitted with a screened doorway. And, if it is a sizeable unit, it should also have a screened window in the back to permit a through-draft.

Best by far is fiberglass screening, although when incorrectly stitched, it sometimes tears loose along the edges. Plastic screening is also used by some tentmakers. Old fashioned cotton mosquito netting still enjoys wide use but it is being muscled out of the game by the improved meshes.

A zippered doorway is more convenient than the "mosquito bar" which must be lifted upon entry or exit, and rolled and tied at the top when not in use.

A light zipper will not stand the abuse of being operated hastily, under stress, or by kids. Make certain your tent is fitted with a heavy-duty zipper. Nylon or metal zippers are both satisfactory.

The nylon zipper never needs lubrication and, of course, is impervious to rust. A quick rub with beeswax or candle grease will keep metal zippers zipping.

Other features to watch for when tent shopping are straight, tight, heavy stitching, lap-felled (folded) seams, side eaves to shed rain, and fabric quality.

A tent is not an annual purchase. When you spend a lot of money for a camping shelter, you expect it to stand up to years of use (and abuse) and still remain water repellent.

Some poor quality cotton ducks on the market are stiffened with sizing which will vanish after repeated drenchings and sunnings, leaving you with a limp, wet tent. Therefore, you are better off buying a good tent in the beginning.

My own preference is Egyptian cotton, sometimes called "sail silk". It has more than 200 per square inch. My tents made from this fabric have remained weathertight over the years, without any supplementary waterproofing.

Ventile is an even better material, with a thread count per square inch in excess of 350.

Most tents are water-resistant when purchased. Some waterproofing compounds which must be applied with a brush will add pounds to the weight of your shelter. The silicone sprays work well and weigh less. Small leaks can be plugged by rubbing a candle over the bad spots.

How about nylon? It is as tough as a pig's nose, shower-roof, mildew resistant and lightweight. But it has a big drawback. It does not breathe. You have probably noticed this with nylon shirts or jackets which become uncomfortably clammy in hot weather.

Thus, you will have condensation problems with nylon tents unless they are well-ventilated.

While plastics have been a great boon to the camping fraternity in many ways, those big polyethylene sheets which some people cart on wilderness trips are a curse. And I will go so far as to say that they should be banned.

A polyethylene sheet makes a very bad tent which does not breathe at all, hence the interior is soon coated with moisture. These are a dangerous fire hazard — hang a lantern close to a piece of plastic and you will see what I mean.

But what happens when it's time to break camp that makes me boil. Nothing happens, that's what. The crudely erected shelter stays right there. After all, who wants to roll up that wet, greasy, torn sheet and take it home?

So, it becomes an ugly, indestructible, perpetual blight on the outdoors and so another beautiful landscape has been defiled.

One of the most versatile items in the camper's kit is a flysheet, which has a multitude of uses.

With a flysheet, the tent will remain cooler in summer and warmer in winter. And it will keep the shelter's interior and the occupants' exteriors dry during violent or steady rainstorms.

A flysheet also converts into an excellent windbreak, or a tarp to cover gear left outside, or a roof over your dining area.

But it will do even more if you buy it with tying tapes attached, or have them sewn on later. The flysheet I use has sixteen tapes around the perimeter and another five tapes on the surface. It easily fashions into an excellent lean-to or pup tent. Measuring ten feet by ten feet, yet weighing only two and a half pounds, it rolls into a tiny bundle for packing.

Remember, tents shrink when wet, so during inclement weather shorten poles, and slacken ropes.

If you drive to your destination, it is an excellent idea to bring along a second tent. It can be utilized as an annex for the children, or as a storage room, as a toilet, or as a dressing room.

Few tents come with suitable pegs. The best pegs are V-shaped spring steel which hold best and lie flattest. Serrated nylon and metal pegs are also satisfactory, but wooden pegs have become as extinct as the dodo.

THE BED

While the bough bed will do in a pinch, nowadays I rarely expose myself to pinching. Also long gone is the time when luxury meant a straw or leaf-filled tick. Never heard of one? A tick is the covering for a do-it-yourself mattress. When empty, it rolls into a tight bundle for packing. Come nightfall it is filled with whatever stuffing is at hand. When this task is performed after dark, a camper can sometimes sleep with very strange bedfellows.

In those days you had to be able to take your lumps. Nowadays camping has become much more luxurious. There is no dearth of mattresses and cots designed with the camper in mind.

Air mattresses are more popular than foam mattresses and have the biggest following. Most air mattresses are nylon, cotton or drill-covered rubber; and many come with two valves; one for the attached pillow and the other one for the bed portion.

Air mattresses made from plastic are little more than toys, best suited for the beach.

Also, the smaller dimensions of the average plastic mattress fail to provide much of a bed. Being easily punctured, a plastic mattress is no bargain from a durability standpoint.

19

Rubber mattresses should never be pressed into dual service as rafts. Frequent soakings and sunnings will drastically shorten their life span.

There is a wide range of sizes and styles of air mattresses from which to choose. Some even convert into chaise lounges.

Most campers should steer clear of mattresses without attached pillows. Look for extra-large tubes at the edges, which help keep the restless sleeper in his bed. I prefer air mattresses with smaller tubes running crossways between the big tubes.

All the tubes should be the same size if you want to make a double-bed. This is usually done with two identical mattresses which dome together.

I once spent the night on an air mattress which converted into a water bed.

On a wild-river canoe trip the tent we packed was barely adequate. During the night, the foot of my mattress, which had all its tubes running lengthways, poked under the front flap. When it started to rain, the downpour ran off the shelter, onto the mattress and flowed along its grooves. When I awoke, my sleeping bag had acted like a blotter until it was saturated, and my skin was getting that way too.

That proved to be one of the most miserable, sleepless nights of my life, and the next night was not any great shakes either. A full day in the warm sunshine failed to dry the down filling of my sleeping bag.

On a tough pack trip, a hand or foot pump is non-essential gear and should remain at home. Huffing and puffing to fill your bed with hot air may leave you weak and dizzy, but it is worth it not to have to carry a pump on your back.

While good air mattresses are tough, they can be punctured. I have hit rock bottom in the night on several occasions — the dirty work of a stray fishhook in both cases. Sticks, stones or other sharp objects can also make short work of your comfort.

A patching kit is essential. Most kits come with patches too tiny to cover anything bigger than pinpricks. Carry a piece of light rubber, a chunk of old inner tube is fine, to look after rips or long cuts.

Carry a couple of extra plugs. They have a habit of straying unless tied to the unit. If you do lose a plug, you can whittle one from a stick if you are stuck.

Do not over-inflate your mattress or you will be in for an uncomfortable night. The mattress has enough air when it barely keeps you off the ground.

Store your mattress where it is cool, dark and dry. Roll it loosely or, better still, lightly inflate it. Rubber deteriorates in the cold, so do not leave air mattresses in unheated garages, sheds, or cottages if the temperature dips below freezing.

Before purchasing an air mattress, carefully check the inflated size. The dimensions printed on the label are usually the deflated measurements and, when filled with air, the mattress will be several inches shorter and narrower.

My preference in a camp bed is a polyether foam-mattress with a ridged or waffled underside and a smooth top.

Because foam breathes, condensation is rarely a problem. These mattresses are comfortable in summer or winter. In winter the thick foam pad is good insulation against the cold. While they come in various thicknesses, you will be sacrificing comfort if you choose one less than two and a half inches deep.

For people who need to eliminate weight and bulk while camping, the answer is the shorty mattress — either air-filled or foam. This hip-length four-footer is all you really need, since it cushions shoulders, back and buttocks.

Cots are very good for hot-weather comfort. Air circulates around them, and heat escapes through the bottom.

Safari-style cots, with spring steel legs which snap into the frame, are the best bet. The two common complaints about safari-style cots are that they are too short for six-footers and too tippy. If thoughts of the latter upset you, rest assured that you will not have far to fall.

AND BEDDING

Here is a chilling bedtime story.

Joe Doaks, Jill Doaks and the two little Doaks are eagerly looking forward to their first camping adventure. Next-door neighbor has loaned them his tent, they have borrowed brother-in-law's campstove, and Joe has brought home some foam rubber from work, which he has cut into mattresses. All they have to buy are sleeping bags. But four of them constitutes a big expenditure. Naturally, Joe has his eye peeled for a "good deal".

While driving by Shady Sam's Bargain Barn, Joe spots a banner reading "Super Sleeping Bag Savings", so he turns into the parking lot.

Ten minutes later he is on his way home with a back seat full of sleeping bags, anxious to show his family his great buy. "They were a real steal", he exclaims, "two for the price of one!" He points out the features the salesman sold him on.

"Just lift one, it is as light as a feather. And look at this rubber bottom—keeps out the damp you know. How about this jazzy pattern on the lining—wild animals and flying birds. Boy, are these great!"

However, they were disastrous.

The mercury dipped to forty degrees; the Doaks shivered and chattered. Like Joe's head, the bags were stuffed with cotton. Jill complained about the way hers lumped under her spine. The rubber bottoms soon made them clammy, and one of the shoddy zippers on the kids' bags jammed and refused to zip.

"Never again", exlaimed Joe to Jill as they sped homeward early that morning. "Camping's for the birds." His unhappy wife nodded in agreement. The little Doaks had nothing to say. They were catching up on the sleep they had missed the night before.

People by the thousands make the same mistake every day. They don't know that you can't tell a bag by its covering, and only find out when it is too late and their holiday is ruined.

To Joe Doaks, a sleeping bag was a sleeping bag. It did not occur to him to investigate why some cost more than others. He did not think to check into the difference between a summer-weight and winter-weight bag, or to investigate the merits of various fillings.

Several features should always be musts. One, is a sturdy zipper which opens down the side and across the bottom, so that the bag may be spread flat for airing or zipped to another bag to form a double bed. Also, the zipper should be operative either from the inside or the outside.

Some people like dome fasteners, but I am not among them. While I have never owned one myself, I have slept in a number of expensive, sub-zero domed bags supplied by outfitters in the far north as part of a "package" deal. Without exception, they all have had one or more domes pulled through the fabric. However, in a domed bag, a sleeper can leap loose instantly in an emergency.

Rubberized bottoms on sleeping bags are useless. As the Doaks discovered, instead of being a vapor barrier to keep ground moisture outside, the rubber traps condensation inside. On a summer camping trip, this is merely uncomfortable, but condensation can be downright dangerous on an extended snow-camping outing.

Besides that, rubberized bags are hard to dry clean, and most cleaners will either refuse to touch them or will not guarantee the job.

And it is little wonder that Joe's sleeping bags were so light and so cold. They were each filled with a pound of cotton, which has very poor insulating qualities.

While kapok is an improvement on cotton, it is far from good, and should be shunned in favor of one of the polyester fibres, Dacron, or down. A feathers and down combination is quite satisfactory, however synthetics have the advantage of being non-allergenic and mildewproof. And they can almost match down for warmth too.

However, down is still the best in the long run.

It compresses into next-to-nothing, doesn't mat, permits circulation so that the sleeper stays dry, and all it needs to freshen it is a shake or two. While down is only one-quarter of the weight of wool, it has four times the insulating qualities.

Summer-weight bags contain as little as one pound

of down, whereas sub-zero models may be stuffed with up to five pounds. Of course, the ideal for extra cold weather is a double bag, one inside the other.

While it is advisable to keep a sleeping bag open and hanging while in storage, I have found that a few minutes of shaking and fluffing will bring even the tightest-rolled down bag back to life again.

The covering of the bag may be one of many fabrics; poplin, nylon, sailcloth or other quality cottons.

How the insulation is stitched into the bag is important. The worst insulating technique is straight quilting, where the outer and inner shells are sewn into "pockets" to contain the filling. Naturally, this type of construction laces the sleeping robe with cold veins.

Best of all is the wall, or overlapping tube quilting. Material is sewn between the outer and inner shells to eliminate these chilly areas.

The size and shape of a sleeping bag are important. If you are bigger than the average person in length and/ or girth, then the standard bag is not for you. Get an extra-large model, and you will be forever grateful that you did. My own preference is a barrel-shaped bag.

Most common of all are the ordinary rectangular shapes, followed by the "mummy" designs for small sleepers not prone to tossing and turning.

What about pillows? Some campers bring pillows from home, which is fine if you have the space. Many people have them built on to their air mattresses, and still others carry small inflatable pillows. I generally pack a pillowcase which I stuff with a sweater or other clothing.

Whatever type of sleeping bag you choose, make

sure that it is good quality. You would not settle for shoddy bedding at home; the same guidelines apply in camp.

APPLIANCES

Stoves

Food cooked over a wood fire always tastes better, or so it seems. When the time and the situation are right, an open fire always adds a touch of charm to an outdoors meal. The stone barbecues at many state and provincial campgrounds are next-best.

However, the camp stove is a godsend as far as convenience is concerned. It is also wonderful during or following rain, when dry firewood is at a premium.

Easily the most popular stove is the two-burner model which burns naphtha gas. The leading camp-stove manufacturer estimates that twenty-five million are in operation in North America. They fold into a "suitcase" for toting, and when opened, the lid and a pair of hinged flaps act as wind baffles.

They are available in three-burner models too, with the extra element boosting size, weight and price.

These are tough units and can take a lot of punishment with very little maintenance. The pressure in the fuel tank must be kept up by periodic pumping. I have found, that possibly due to filling through a filtered funnel and occasionally oiling the washer on the pump, mine has never given me any trouble, and I have yet to replace a single part.

People who drive to their camp site, and especially the dishwasher who is sick and tired of cleaning blackened pots and pans, should seriously consider getting a propane-burning campstove.

While propane is more expensive than naphtha,

it is clean and convenient — no mess, fuss, pumping or fuel-spilling.

The large refillable container takes a fair bite out of the pocketbook at the outset, but it is the best buy in the long run.

If you use the small throw away cylinders or cans, never pitch them into the fire. They go "kaboom!" and are very dangerous missiles. Dispose of them in the campground rubbish containers, bury them, or bring them home to your local garbage collector.

The spark lighter is the key to quick ignition, and you do not run the risk of getting your fingers burned or your beard singed.

A stove stand is also a "must". It supports the unit firmly at a height which most chefs find ideal.

Since it is important to keep your campstove level, the stand will accomplish this. On soft ground the legs can be pushed into the soil, and on rocks they can be leveled with the help of flat stones.

A griddle which sits above the burners is a worthwhile acquisition. Having a large, flat surface and grease wells, it is ideal for frying bacon, eggs, fish, etc.

Another accessory which some people will appreciate, is a box-shaped oven which fits on top of a burner. Some ovens are rigid, but others fold flat for packing. Most of them have heat gauges, so there is no reason why the camp cook cannot feed her ravenous brood succulent roasts and mouth-watering cakes and pies.

While these stoves are too bulky for the backpacker and canoe tripper, there are good quality one-burner stoves which occupy no more than a few square inches of precious pack space.

The most compact are small, inexpensive, folding

types which burn solid fuel or "canned heat". My choice is a tiny naphtha burner with a half-pint fuel tank.

Even at the campground, one of these very small stoves is handy for making coffee or keeping soup hot while the rest of the meal is being prepared on the larger stove.

Lanterns and Lights

While there are more than twice as many stoves as lanterns in use among North America's camping fraternity, if I had to choose between a lantern or a stove, I would without hesitation choose a lantern.

The naphtha-burning lanterns generally are better than propane-burning because of lower operational costs and portability around the campsite. They are also handier for hanging inside a tent.

Many campers find themselves in a quandary; whether to buy a single or a double-mantle lantern. It is interesting to note that the most popular single-mantle model has 350 candlepower, whereas a double-mantle lantern provides only an additional 50 candlepower.

I prefer the single-mantle model with 550 candlepower. If you are careful to pack your lantarn in one of the specially-built boxes, you will not be greeted by a broken globe or ruined mantle when you reach your destination.

Always carry an extra globe, well-wrapped to protect the glass. And never venture forth without at least two spare mantles.

To avoid grief with plugged, fouled generators, fill the lantern's fuel tank through a funnel which has a felt pad covering a fine screen, so as to strain off dirt.

Kerosene lanterns using mantles must be pre-heated, and throw a very weak light. Because kerosene is virtually non-combustible, I once purchased a kerosene lantern in the interests of safety. However, after its first outing it was shelved to the storeroom, where it still is to this day.

Battery lights lack brilliance and warmth, and are not recommended for general use.

Fluorescent lamps which plug into the socket of a vehicle's cigarette lighter throw plenty of light, with little drain on the battery.

When hiking or paddling into the boondocks, all the above might well be scrapped in favor of an old standby—the candle lantern, which throws enough light for reading and takes up next-to-no space. Carry a stack of slow-burning candles.

How many times have you forgotten to pack your flashlight? Everybody does. Also, on several occasions when I flipped the switch, darkness still reigned. Either the batteries had been left inside the flashlight and had leaked, or the switch had been pushed on inside my pack and they had drained en route.

Leaving batteries loose to install at camp is one solution, but, the best thing to do is to simply reverse them inside the flashlight.

A bright multi-cell light has disadvantages too—it is heavier to carry and more costly to operate.

I consider the waterproof two-cell light the most durable, and the best suited to most campers' requirements.

Heaters

Tent heaters are of little use to fair-weather campers. You will find them discussed at some length in the Snow Camping Section. It should be noted that there are four basic types of heaters, which burn wood, alcohol, naphtha and propane.

The propane type is probably the most efficient although its heat radiates in only one direction. It is also expensive to operate.

Wood burners generate a lot of heat, if your tent will adapt to a stovepipe and your camp is more permanent than a one night stand.

Most naphtha catalytic heaters are inadequate if rated at fewer than 5000 B.T.U.'s.

I personally like the Swedish-made alcohol burner which gets hot enough to cook on. It boasts a simple control knob for temperature adjustment by raising or lowering the wick.

Ice Boxes

While most ice boxes can hardly be termed appliances, there are some propane models available which are real refrigerators. The price tag is somewhat prohibitive, except for people who spend all their weekends and vacations in campgrounds, in which case the expense is probably worthwhile. These refrigerators are especially suitable for the tent-trailer crowd.

The refrigerator for most campers is an ice chest or cooler. These come in myriad sizes and qualities. Some styrofoam coolers are available for the price of a "six-pack", while models with metal shells can cost twenty times as much.

The cheap styrofoam type is extremely fragile and even the expensive ones are no great shakes for casual living. They dent with little coaxing which, in turn, may spring a liner or a lid. Also, given time, plus average use and abuse, they will rust.

My top choice is the fiberglass cooler, which is durable and does a good job. Happily, the price tag will not make you gulp.

Fiberglass coolers come in various sizes, but for a family, the forty-two quart model is the best. Remember, much of that space is taken up by a block of ice.

Coolers should be equipped with sturdy handles on the ends, a tray which rests above the ice, and a spigot or plug near the bottom for draining.

Dry ice under the block of ice will make it last much longer. But beware of handling dry ice. Its temperature is minus 109° F, and contact with skin will result in a nasty burn.

Whenever we drive to our destination, and weight and bulk are not a problem, we carry a second cooler, which we place in a pit. This we use for keeping take-home-fish fresh, and as the source of ice for our "sundowners." Who said "campers ain't got no couth"?

AXES, KNIVES, SAWS

The expression "a knife is as good as its edge" does not refer to the length of the blade. There are some very silly-looking daggers to be seen around the campground.

Why anyone would want one of those tapered stilettos is a mystery; their use beyond opening letters or stabbing toads is an even bigger mystery.

Equally puzzling are machetes which dangle from belt to knee. These blades have merit for clearing vines and light brush from the tent site, but that is where their usefulness stops.

A belt knife need not have a blade longer than four

31

inches, five inches maximum. A deep wrap-around sheath covering most of the handle as well as the blade will lessen chances of loss. Many seasoned outdoorsmen insert the belted sheath into a back pocket where it cannot flip-flop and dump its cargo.

The handle should fit your hand, to prevent your fingers slipping against the blade. Otherwise, it should have a guard between the handle and steel.

You will see many bushmen who have only a folding pocket knife for everything from cleaning fish to gutting deer, to just whittling. Jack-knives worn in a belt sheath are also worth considering.

A whetstone is a necessary item in a camper's kit, to be used often for keeping a keen edge on the blade.

Hatchets I would like to dismiss with just a few words. They are of some value to hunters when dressing and hanging game, and are sometimes helpful to campers for such chores as driving nails or tent pegs, but that is where their usefulness ends.

An axe is something else again. It is a functional tool and anyone who makes his pitch off the beaten track should have one on hand.

Steer clear of double-bitted axes which, in inexperienced hands can take a bite from a log on the downstroke and lop off an ear on the return trip.

A splitting axe is best for the average camper, as the thin headed brushing axes will not hack firewood.

The smaller axes with twenty-six inch handles and two pound to two and a half pound heads may do the job in the hands of an expert, but are too short, light and dangerous for the sometime-chopper.

Add a pound to the head and eight inches to the handle, and you have an efficient chopping tool.

Keep your axe safely sheathed when not in use. One of the handiest sheaths which I have seen was affixed on the outside of a pack near its base, and a buckled strap riveted to the top end secured the handle.

Carried in this way, it is there when you need it, not buried inside the pack or kicking around in the canoe where it becomes another handful on a portage.

Axes should be sharpened with a file and the finishing touches should be done with a whetstone.

The small take-down buck saws or miniature versions of the Swede saw are really handy, and will bite through a log "like butter." Big game hunters generally carry a meat blade to insert in the frame.

There are now many ultra-light chain saws for sale which make wood-cutting a game, not a chore. However, a bit of honest sweat has never harmed anyone and, as they also shatter the precious peace of the outdoors, should be shunned.

ODDS AND ENDS

Some sundries are necessities, others are comfort aids, space permitting, while still others fit under the "utter nonsense" heading.

The folding shovel or trenching tool looks more useful than it actually is. I must admit that I have never trenched my tent, nor have I ever wished I had. If you camp at the foot of a hard-packed slope, this might be a worthwhile item. Otherwise, it merely adds to the bulk and weight of your gear.

If you take a mirror with you for shaving or applying makeup, make it metal for obvious reasons. It does scratch easily, so keep it in a cloth bag or hang it on a tree.

An insulated vacuum-bottle is useful when making field or fishing trips. The wide-mouthed bottle is excellent for thick soups, as well as cold or hot drinks. If weight is not a problem, the stainless steel bottle is well worth its big price tag. It is unbreakable and, unless dropped in the path of a steamroller, will last a lifetime.

A canteen goes under the "necessity" heading. Be sure to buy a felt-covered canteen, as its contents will remain cool due to evaporation, if dipped occasionally in water.

Canvas or plastic folding buckets are practical for hauling water from a pump, a stream or a lake. Also excellent water carriers are collapsible clear five-gallon polythene water jugs, equipped with spigots. Place one on the edge of a table or flat surface, and you will have the convenience of water "on tap".

If you drive to your campsite, go by boat, or even fly, if you have enough room for canvas folding chairs, take them, by all means. It is sheer luxury to sink into a chair beside the campfire after a day in the woods or on the water.

There are even folding chairs-and-table kits available. They make a heavy, bulky package, so they are only practical if you drive to your campsite.

Always take a tiny sewing kit with you for emergency repairs.

Another amenity is the portable "john", which folds compactly for packing. It will come with "throwaway" bags, which might be better referred to as "disposable." Remember to take several packages of extra bags.

Portable showers rate in my "nonsense" division. How much better it is to dive into a lake or a river, wash in a stream, or have a companion pour a pail of water over your head!

Garbage bags are useful in many ways, besides the purpose for which they were designed. They will protect you and your loose gear in case of a downpour. They are ideal for sealing cameras or clothing during canoe trips. But their most important use is to stash litter and garbage to bring back with you.

If everyone did that, campsites would be more pleasant places.

THE KITCHEN

Equip yourself for camp cooking and dining at your nearest outfitting or sporting goods store, not in your home kitchen. The pots, pans, utensils and dinnerware will not be as fancy as those found in your drawers and cupboards, but they will be more durable and less expensive.

You will see many self-contained "kitchens" in the campgrounds, most of them home-made from plywood, incorporating the ideas and designs of the individual cooks. When opened, the kitchens have sides or fronts which convert into work tables or counters. Inside, there is a place for everything, and everything is in its place.

There is a drawer or pouch for cutlery, a shelf for dishes and another for pots and pans. Salt, pepper and sundry condiments are all secure and at hand.

It goes without saying that such a kitchen is out of the question for the wilderness camper, who must forego such luxury in favor of minimum weight and bulk.

When searching for a nest of billies or a family-sized mess kit, you may be hard-pressed to find good quality cookware. Too many manufacturers seem to be of the opinion that the camper is a bargain hunter who will happily settle for shoddy gear if the price is right. Any serious camper has discovered on his early outings that quality is the best buy in the long run, and he is willing to pay the price to get it.

Most mess kits are poorly designed. The plates are too small, the frying pan is inadequate, and the cups are punched out of aluminum and so retain enough heat to sear your lips long after the contents has cooled.

These should be thrown out and replaced with plastic or melmac mugs. The dinner plates should be exchanged for some with a generous twelve-inch diameter and a high rim to contain the stews and baked beans which are common camp fare.

Choose a cast iron frying pan, unless the weight factor is important.

While many campsites have several metal grills "in residence", they cannot be counted on. Bring your own, either a grill with folding legs or one which you have rescued from an old ice box or refrigerator. They become very sooty, so make a cotton bag for storage.

Often forgotten are a pot lifter, an egg flipper, an oven mitt and even can and bottle openers. Many a knife sports nicks from service as a replacement for the left-at-home can opener.

The knife-fork-spoon sets which snap together as a compact unit are excellent for both wilderness and campground use.

Unless you prefer your eggs scrambled, carry them in a rigid plastic or aluminum container.

Folding pyramid toasters work well on the grill over a campstove or open fire.

If space permits, bring along a coffee pot. If not, brew it in a billy or settle for the instant variety.

And don't forget that a roll of tin foil has a multitude of uses.

Chapter Two

CAMP LORE

WHERE WHY AND HOW TO MAKE YOUR PITCH

It was a beautiful awakening. Brilliant sunshine streamed through the screened doorway and every bird greeted the new day with a joyful song. Wife and Babe slept peacefully as I crept through the flap out into the grassy clearing ablaze with windflowers, their open faces turned skyward. There was not an insect on that picturesque plateau, and the light dew which had descended during the night had served to accentuate the green of the grass and emphasize the good smells of the earth.

I splashed my face with gin-clear water from the icy brook which tumbled down the slope only paces from the tent. It met the sparkling blue lake after a final frothy fling as a miniature waterfall.

The scene was breathtaking. The sun bathed the green clad slopes in golden light and glittered on the ice cream mountain tops.

It was our private domain. There wasn't another soul as far as the eye could see.

As the lake beyond the white sand cove began to

dimple with rising fish, I scrambled back to the tent for my flyrod. Three casts later a trio of chunky, brightly-painted Kamloops trout flopped in the ferns.

In minutes I had gathered enough driftwood for a crackling fire, filletted those trout, and began to prepare the breakfast of my life.

Sounds like a dream campsite you say? Well, you're right on target. I awoke just as those succulent fillets started to sizzle.

You won't find many campsites like that one, at least not on this side of the Great Divide.

But too many people keep vainly looking until day's end when they're greeted by the "Campground Filled" sign or, at best, must settle for a last ditch stand that is either far removed from the facilities or virtually on top of them.

To be far from the madding crowd is the desire of most campers, rating high on the list of reasons why they were initially attracted to tenting or trailering.

But it can sometimes be a large order. While the proximity of campers is not too oppressive in most state and provincial parks where overcrowding is carefully avoided by the authorities, the same cannot be said of some privately owned tent and trailer parks whose unscrupulous owners often ignore ethics and regulations when the business bucket brims over.

You will stand a good chance of finding a choice site if you wrap up your day on the road by mid-aftertoon.

This gives you an opportunity to scout the campground and select a site which fills the bill on at least some of your requisites.

You will want to be set-up where you won't be

plagued by hordes of insects. Ideally, this would be on high ground away from the swamps and stagnant ponds which are mosquito havens. Long grass and underbrush should be trimmed or absent for the same reason.

While tenting beside a fast-flowing stream may be aesthetically appealing, that happens to be where you'll encounter the greatest concentration of black flies. It's logical, because that's where the beggars lay their eggs.

Bugs don't like to battle a breeze, so if your camp has a windward exposure, you will have less grief with those critters.

Ideally, this exposure should be to the east. Thus the morning sun will dry the dew, awaken you far more gently than the blankety-blank alarm clock, and will soon chase the chills from your bedroom.

It is also desirable to find a site with trees along its westerly boundary, offering a shady respite from the afternoon sun. On a still day, a tent in the hot sun will become an oven and roast its occupants.

If the roof is unavoidably exposed to direct sunshine, a flysheet is a big help in keeping the tent liveable.

Finding the ideal location presents more of a problem in campgrounds than out beyond, where the woods and lakeshores are all yours.

What could be more idyllic than pitching beside a waterfall, just as on the postcards? Try it some night and I guarantee you'll have the answer by morning.

Your campsite, your tent and possibly you, will be soaking wet. "It's a great place to visit but I wouldn't want to live there".

Naturally, the lower the ground, the greater the drenching by dewdrops. Near water level next to a lake can be a bad choice too.

Beaches have other disadvantages. A night on deep soft sand can result in a stiff sore back. Also, the stuff gets into everything from larder to lingerie.

Avoid the heavy traffic areas in campgrounds. This means beside showers, lavatories, community kitchen, general store, docks, etc. Also, steer clear of the main roads, which are frequently dusty and noisy.

While incompatible neighbors are sometimes unavoidable, it is often easy to pre-judge people by the camp they keep.

If the equipment is of decent quality, the site neat and well laid out, then the tenants are good campers, which usually means that they're good folks too. However, remember that this is not an infallible rule-of-thumb.

Some of the best campground neighbors I've bumped into were holidaying midst a shambles of gear, food, and whatever. And don't discount the guy who greets the new day with a beer and a belch. There is a good chance that he's a big-hearted slob who sips away all day, and quietly sacks out at nightfall.

Everyone enjoys a late and boisterous party at times, but not when your campground neighbors inconsiderately keep you and yours awake half the night. Yelping dogs and yapping youngsters can also cause insomnia.

Small islands can be fun to camp on, and often offer privacy, good shore fishing, no bugs and no ring-tailed grub thieves. But if you are on a well traveled canoe route, you may find that all the firewood has long ago gone up in smoke.

Speaking of canoe tripping, don't camp right on

the portage trail or plumb against the launching or landing "pad." The kindred souls you meet en route are frequently solitude-seekers who shun tent cities. But you will find them helpful, interesting and willing to help or advise.

A final word of caution. Don't pitch under leaning trees, or those with dead limbs.

On a fly-in moose hunt to an isolated lake, the guides went in on the first flight to set up camp, while the pilot returned for us, dropping us into that small body of water at dusk. By the time we had unpacked and had supper, we were ready to turn in. The wind sprang up during the night and I awoke to the sound of creaking and groaning above out heads. Investigation showed the guides had foolishly pitched in the path of a massive birch tree which leaned dangerously at a forty-five degree angle. My companion and I decided that we would not sleep another wink unless we switched our diggings to a safer location; and we did there and then.

Shortly before dawn we were startled into wakefulness by a thundering crash. Yes, the tree's final moment had arrived, and it had come to rest right across the spot where the tent had been standing. Had we still been inside, it would have put us six-feet under, literally and figuratively speaking.

Manitou keeps an eye on campers.

BEATING THE BUGS

The bush is bugged, and getting into a sweat over it makes matters worse. When repellent drips away with perspiration, your problems are compounded by the fact that some insects, notably black flies, are attracted to wet skin.

The black fly heads most hate-lists, and only foolishly intrepid campers venture into the northern United States and Canadian wilderness in May, June or July without preparing for encounters with clouds of these boring, bloodsucking critters. The farther north you travel the later the black fly "season".

They're at their worst in the vicinity of running water, and get especially vicious before and after a rain shower. Muggy days are bad ones. They disappear after sunset, to give their victims a respite in which to lick their wounds before the next day's battle begins.

Even when they aren't "feeding", they can drive a man almost mad by crawling in eyes, ears and nose. Open your mouth for a second and you can chomp on a dozen. If you have never encountered the black fly, you will be surprised by its dimunitiveness. It is not much larger than no-see-'ems.

The scourge has been known to goad cattle into frenzied stampedes, and will drive moose to water more surely than a pack of hounds.

While I've heard of no human deaths from their bites, I wouldn't be surprised if there are cases on record. Many have been hospitalized following severe attacks, and I have come close to it myself. Years ago I returned from the bush so badly chewed that I was feverish, and my neck and wrists were swollen to the point I couldn't button shirt cuffs or collar.

Black fly bites are also highly infectious. One developed into a boil which spread its poison through my system, and kept recurring for almost a year.

Pretty scary? Perhaps my bark is worse than their bite.

And their bites may look worse than they are. Black

flies inject an anti-coagulant into the wound, so their prey (that's us) may bleed profusely.

With proper preparation and precautions they can be kept at bay. You might even return to civilization virtually unscathed, except for a few wounds from sporadic sniping.

A doctor suggested that the answer to my plight might be Vitamin B1, expounding the theory that they find those deficient in this vitamin especially mouth-watering. To my surprise, it worked. In late winter and early spring I get my system built up with several injections. While they don't find me totally repulsive, the number of bites I collect is minimal.

I have met only one other person who subscribes to the same ounce of prevention, and he is equally loud in his praise. He swallows B1 in pill form for several weeks before heading for the boondocks.

As with most drugs and medication, check with your doctor before trying this prescription.

Some repellents do a fair job of keeping the black fly out of range, but smoke is by far the best. Traveling through northwoods communities when this vampire is in high gear, you will see many homes with smudge pots spewing in their yards or on their porches. They're effective. So is a pipe, cigar or, to a lesser degree, cigarettes.

By sealing off the access points at wrists, neck and ankles, you'll certainly diminish the black fly feeding grounds. Tuck trousers into boots or thick socks, wear a turtle neck sweater or neck bandana, and a shirt, jacket or sweater with elasticised or knit cuffs.

Wear a hat and, if they get really mean, don a headnet.

When and where insects are a problem, if possible

camp on a breezy knoll, point of land, or island.

Mosquitoes aren't nearly as difficult to deal with, being more easily deterred by the anti-bug sprays and lotions. But because they frequent more southerly climes, the same amount of protective clothing usually can't be worn.

Sprays are the easiest to apply, but don't squirt them directly into your face. Spray repellent into your palm, then apply it by hand, taking care to avoid eyes and mouth.

Some repellents destroy rubber, varnish, plastics and certain paints. Anglers have had expensive tackle boxes ruined when a bottle leaked or spilled. Hunters have found the finish from their guns stuck to their palms. And bush workers have actually had their hard hats deteriorate.

Having tested some 7000 insect-repelling chemicals, the United States Department of Agriculture reported Deet (diethyl-meta-toluamide) protected the wearer twice as long as others. It's found in a number of popular brands, and the percent per volume should be printed on the label.

It is said mosquitoes find those with a high sugar content in their systems desirable fare. Bananas are a no-no, although citrus fruits help repel them.

While those of us who have co-existed with mosquitoes all our lives have developed a certain degree of immunity, the same is not true of people who hail from European countries where there are no mosquitoes.

A few bites can make them really ill. Each bite may swell like a hornet sting, and limbs may become puffed and angry-looking, similar to blood poisoning. In such cases, take them to a doctor or hospital without delay. Antibiotics could be required.

Did you know that dark colored clothing will attract both mosquitoes and black flies, whereas light shades can shy them away? It's a fact. Leave the black, purple, navy and maroon at home.

Apply repellents with frequency, especially in hot weather.

Spray your jacket, trousers and hat with a powerful garden bug killer, taking great care not to get it on your skin. It's also a good idea to give the inside of the tent a few squirts, an hour or two before retiring, to ensure a restful night's sleep.

Fine screening is a must, mostly for mosquitoes. Black flies may get inside your trailer, tent or car, but they rarely bite when indoors.

Shun perfumed deodorants and after-shave lotions. Smelly old bushmen don't need karate lessons to keep the belles at bay, but what matters most to them is that the insects find them equally unappealing.

Those itching chiggers or redbugs are turned off by repellents, as are bees and wasps. Don't count on your sprays and lotions doing any good if you walk into one of their cone-shaped domiciles or squat on the entrance to their underground nest.

Deer fly bites hurt like blazes. I've never found anything to beat them, except a quick slap. They won't be shooed, and you have to squash the life out of them before they give up.

Ticks are loathsome creatures, and you will feel positively unclean if you discover one buried in your hide. It will be difficult, but resist the urge to brush them off. Touch their backs with a lighted cigarette or a match and they will pull out on their own. But if you try to yank one loose, its infectious head may remain behind.

You may not know that the male mosquito is not in

the people-eating business. In fact, the harmless little fellow subsists entirely on plant juices, and only the female of the species goes on jugular junkets.

FIREMAKING

There's a great deal to be said for a campfire, aside from warmth and light.

Here is where one can come to terms with oneself and with life. While gazing into the flickering flames, worries dissolve, problems are solved, and peace of mind takes over.

There is a bit of the dreamer and philosopher in even the most case-hardened character. These qualities may have been shoved into the nethermost corner of the brain by the pandemonium of today's lifestyle, but they often surface at the fireside.

I have shared a sundowner and a campfire with businessmen who have just stepped off the treadmill. They liken their daily pace to running up the "down" escalator; if they stop for a breath they will find themselves at the bottom again. After a few hours in camp they were like new men. They no longer talked shop, they laughed as if they meant it, and they recalled happy experiences from the misty past, which hadn't entered their heads in years. Camping might be sounder therapy than the headshrinker's couch.

While Jimmy, my woods-wise Indian guide, elected to brew a billy of tea, I stood beside the beached canoe and made a dozen "last casts" in the promising slick at the head of the rapids. "Want to see an old Indian firemaking trick?" my companion asked.

"Hooray", thought I "a demonstration of the age-old bow or drill friction technique." As I eagerly watched, he laughed with glee, pulled his lighter out of his pocket and, presto, fire flickered in the tiny pile of tinder. Another city slicker slickered!

Joking aside, a lighter makes good sense as an emergency firelighter, being impervious to rain and dunking. If you carry one, keep it filled and attached to a belt loop with cord, thong or strong elastic.

A "metal match", basically a flint which is struck with steel to produce a firelighting spark, is a worthwhile item, as is a waterproof match box. The match box I favor is cruder and more effective. I paraffin a box of wooden kitchen matches, which I stash in a pocket of the pack. Now the block of matches is totally waterproof, and individual sticks may be pried loose when needed.

Even many seasoned outdoorsmen tote a few homemade paraffined firestarting aids for days when tinder is scarce or soaking wet. The backyard barbecue revolution has been responsible for the introduction of some excellent products. One, which comes in jelly form in a squeeze tube, has the added feature of doubling as an emergency torch. Among the best, are solid white cubes made from a petroleum byproduct. Each weighs only two thirds of an ounce.

As most people know, birch bark is the top tinder in the woods. Most living trees have ragged strips dangling from them, and the outer and middle barks girdling the fallen remains of dead birches are generally dry and inflammable. Cedar bark is next best.

Dead leaves, dry pine needles and grass will all do the trick as well.

A traditional bit of tinder is a soft wood stick which has been "slivered" from end to end with the blade of a knife. The slices are left attached, and the result is a stick covered with shavings. These are called fire sticks, fuzz sticks or prayer sticks.

It does not matter what you call them, they work, which is all that counts. If you shove one end in the ground with the stick upright, stack a tepee of fine kindling around it, put a match to it, you are in business.

Before building a fire, selecting a safe site is important.

Do it on a rock, sand or firm soil which has been scraped clean of twigs, leaves, and other ground cover. Do the same thing with a surrounding safety circle.

Never light a fire on peat, leafmold or other humus.

The fellow who does, might read of a blaze over his morning coffee and comment to his wife "There was a forest fire right where we were last weekend. Probably some careless smoker". Yet, he may well be the culprit. Fire can creep underground for hours or days, finally bursting into the open as the beginning of a full-fledged conflagration which could destroy miles of wilderness before it is brought under control.

When you venture forth in the outdoors, you are honor bound to safeguard the heritage which also belongs to millions of others. With cigarettes and fires, exercise caution and common sense at all times.

Always sit down to smoke, break your spent match in two and make sure that it is out. Grind the life out of cigarette and cigar butts until they are definitely dead.

Surround the fireplace with stones, as insurance against the fire ground spreading. Do not build it under overhanging branches or you could set an entire tree ablaze.

Lousy firemakers are usually too anxious to get the

show on the road. Their efforts are often stifled before they have had a chance to really catch on. Think of someone gasping for air and give a young fire room to breathe. Don't smother it with wood and kindling before it gets its start in life.

It is commonsense to ignite a campfire from the upwind side. Yet many a neophyte fusses and cusses because the doggone blaze will not start from a leeward light.

When the tinder is burning, add kindling piece by piece until you have a blaze that is ready for firewood.

Kindling is abundant around most campsites. The branches of fallen trees and the dead lower limbs of pines are ideal. If neither is available, then split a log into kindling-size sticks. Use fast-burning softwoods such as pine, cedar and poplar.

In many government parks and private campgrounds, firewood is supplied. Learn to recognize the different woods; it will help you to build the kind of fire which best suits your needs, be it for cooking, drying, warmth or merely atmosphere.

I personally look for driftwood when it is time to gather fuel. It has been baked by the hot sun until it is thoroughly dry, it burns cleanly, brightly and cheerily, and much of it comes in convenient campfire lengths. One drawback is that it usually disappears too fast.

When searching the forest for firewood, try to find some which has died on the stump or has fallen across rocks or other logs which have kept it off the ground.

The fast and hot burning softwoods include poplar, pine, basswood, cedar and spruce. Oak, hickory, ash, beech, maple, birch, and larch or tamarack are among the most popular hardwoods. These are best suited to all-night fires (usually an exercise in futility) or when a bed of hot coals is required for cooking.

A reflector fire is the efficient way to heat an open tent or lean-to. Unless you are fortunate enough to have a ready-made reflector in the form of a big boulder or rock face, you will have to make one.

Build a wall of green logs, held in position by driving forked stakes into the ground, propping two others into the crotch at an angle, and then piling the logs on these.

If the depth of soil is sufficient, the upright supports may be driven into the ground at a slant, making the second set of stakes unnecessary.

Build the fire a foot or more from the reflector wall.

The most common open-fire cooking set-up features a keyhole arrangement, the stone-supported grill straddling the narrow end. Build a hot fire downwind in the wide portion of the "keyhole", then rake coals from it into the cooking area.

Finally, make certain your fire is dead out. Drown it, stir the ashes, then drown it again. If you are beside water, toss the half-burned logs into the lake or river.

BE WEATHERWISE

Rain can be the bane of campers, but this need not be so. The camper who fishes ignores or even welcomes it. Feed washed into a river or stream will ignite his quarry's hunger pangs, and raindrops on the lake's surface inject oxygen which gives lethargic fish a new lease on life.

However, everyone isn't an angler. A lengthy downpour often spells misery and/or boredom, especially for kids. Games, books, snoozes are all fine pastimes, but not in more than one-day doses.

A lantern or heater perking inside your tent will banish dampness. Stormbound life is much more pleasant in a large tent rather than cooped inside a backpacker's special.

A flysheet can be rigged as a dining or cooking shelter, or set up simply to break the wind and shed the rain. Many campgrounds have recreation centres which are welcome in such weather. If the nearest town isn't too far distant, make a day of it with shopping, a movie and a meal. You will also escape the smug looks from the trailer and motorhome set.

If you must be outdoors, rain or shine, as is the case on a tightly scheduled canoe trip or hike, then proper clothing is vital.

Rainwear runs the gamut from a plastic garbage bag with a hole for your head, to suits worn by mountaineering experts which cost more than your double-breasted pinstripe.

Between these extremes there are coats, suits and ponchos in vinyl and modestly-priced rubberized nylon.

Look for a material which resists ripping when snagged. Check ventilation features. A good arrangement is a mesh lining across the back and shoulders, with the exterior waterproof material overlapping and loose at the bottom, allowing air to circulate and keeping you dry.

Pivot shoulders are another plus. Two-piece combinations are handiest in most situations, although a poncho is best for boat fishing and is also the favorite of many pack-packers. It doubles as a shelter in an emergency and some ponchos are designed with a hump to cover the pack on your back.

Color is of little consequence, but yellow, red and orange will brighten an otherwise dreary day. Yellow also helps shoo the flies and mosquitoes. These colors are also good choices for safety-conscious campers.

"What about an umbrella?" Ahem—and what about it?

The rubber hats worn by Atlantic fishermen—called sou'westers—are sensible headgear in a heavy downpour. A wide-brimmed felt fedora which has been siliconed does a good job too.

Wear a wool shirt, sweater and socks if it's cold. Wool keeps you warm, even when wet.

And if your clothes get soaked, they will have to be dried again, probably beside a fire. Avoid jack pine when stoking a drying fire. It sprinkles your clothing with a layer of soot. Poplar and tamarac are two of the hottest and cleanest burning woods.

When the sun shines again, spread clothing, sleeping bags and whatever else is damp on top of the bushes or a brush pile. The air circulation hastens drying.

Beware of thunderstorms. Get off the water as soon as you can, and don't seek shelter beneath the tallest tree in the forest, or under one on a hilltop or in the middle of a clearing.

Your car is the safest place during an electrical storm. But not if it is parked beside a tall tree, as we once discovered. My fishing companion and I were several miles upriver when the horizon blackened and growled ominously.

We retraced our route, paddling furiously back down that serpentine stream, reaching the safety of the car parked by a bridge just as the heavens opened. A tall pine stood about twenty feet from the road.

Suddenly there was an ear-splitting crack as lightning struck the tree, ran down its entire length, and split it open. Chips of wood exploded in every direction.

Branches and chunks of pine up to three feet in length showered the car. Had we sought shelter under that tree, I probably would not be here to write about it.

A few precautions to take in case of a thunderstorm include covering your campstove and larder, loosening the guy ropes on the tent, tarping your firewood or heaping it under a table, boat or other shelter.

Never pitch on a beach near the water's edge, or on a sandspit in the river. Waves, tides or flood waters could spell calamity.

It helps to be able to predict weather conditions with a measure of accuracy. Of course, always check long-range forecasts before leaving home and tune in to local radio reports, if possible.

There is no dearth of catchy rhymes to help in calling the shots. The angler's poem: "When the wind's from the east the fish bite the least. When it blows from the west, fishing is best" rings with truth.

So does this mariner's barometer: "A red sky at night is a sailor's delight. A red sky at morning is a sailor's warning".

A rosy sunset announces that a fine morrow is in the offing, but when the sun rises in a crimson globe you can bet your britches it won't be visible for long.

A ring around the moon, or a haloed sun are signs that a storm is brewing.

Even the most urbanized camper can recognize obvious indications such as mountainous thunderheads heaped on the horizon.

But it is the more subtle omens which give you time

to prepare for the onslaught.

The south wind, the east wind, or a combination, are frequent bearers of wet tidings.

Sea birds will stay on or near land when a storm is en route. Also, keep an eye on the smoke from your fire. If it travels upwards, then flattens, hovers and drifts back down, the barometer is plummetting too.

It is possible to smell approaching rain, and it can be felt in arthritic joints, bunions and corns. My right hand is a pretty fair barometer.

Rain, winds, or cold need not dampen your spirits on your outing. Be prepared for the worst and, remember, you can't outfight the weather.

A bantamweight doesn't slug it out with a heavyweight. He compensates for the mismatch with nimble footwork and by rolling with the punches.

The same rules apply when you are in the ring with the weatherman.

Chapter Three

FAMILY CAMPING

CAMPING ON WHEELS

How times have changed! Grandma never had it this good — not by a long shot. *Life in the Woods*, published around 1860, counsels the nineteenth century hiking buff, "If you find the opportunity, wash your feet in salt water a week before starting."

Those plagued by bugs were advised to "rub your face and hands with salve or oil mixed with tar". What a way to keep a schoolgirl complexion!

Campers were not forgotten when advice was passed out. The author let it be known he couldn't tolerate tomfoolery and admonished those so inclined, "Have no larking or rough play, as you will, should you camp out long enough, have need of all your strength."

Nowadays, the ultimate in camping convenience and comfort comes on wheels, and you will find wheeler dealers anxious to extol the merits of everything from a $350 tent trailer to a $35,000 motor home.

The tent trailer has many pluses for the average guy with two or three weeks annual vacation.

Tent campers have two basic differences—some come with hard tops, others with soft. Both are built on a box mounted over an axle and wheels.

The canvas-topped models are more economical, while offering most of the features found in those with metal or fiberglass roofs.

They are supported by metal frames which quickly fold out when erecting. All have at least two beds, and some boast zip-on rooms or accordion-like additions, so as many as eight people may sleep in one. All are equipped with a table and benches or bunks. A stove and icebox are standard equipment in many models.

The deluxe version often has this equipment as standard "built ins". The metal or fiberglass top gives a feeling of permanency. Being constructed of fiberglass, plastic or aluminum, it has some features not found with canvas roofs, both when erected and when lowered for travel.

Why is it a good deal for the average family? It is easy to tow, hard-tops provide a solid base on which to lash a canoe or punt, the bedding and other gear stowed inside is safe and dry, and there is no vision obstruction for the car's rear view mirror. There is no necessity for big extension mirrors, nor weight equalizers.

Also, being low it is not as prone to buffeting by cross winds or passing trucks and buses.

Finally, tent trailers do not present quite the same storage problems as do travel trailers; and are not as likely to be ticked off by borough by-laws which dictate where they may not be parked.

If your tent trailer does not have enough space to accommodate mom, dad and the kids in comfort, tote a tent as a bunkhouse for small fry.

The truck camper is a perfect set-up for the vacationer or sportsman on the move. Many times we have wheeled along "goat trails" with hair pin turns which preclude towing a trailer. Thus, we have been able to camp within a fly-cast of a secluded lake or a fast-rushing wild river.

It is not recommended for passengers to ride in the back. However, this is often unavoidable since most trucks lack a back seat. In this case, there should be an intercom to permit communication between driver and passengers. I shudder whenever I pass one of these units and see small faces peering out of a window. Without the benefit of solid seats and seat belts, they are vulnerable to injury in case of a collision or blow out.

Many deluxe truck campers boast all the comforts of home: stove, refrigerator, toilet, shower, air conditioning, heating, and lights.

You will probably drive your truck camper over rough terrain, so dishes, pans, bottles or food will take off unless cupboards are securely latched. Be neat. Never leave loose gear or other items lying about.

At the campsite, the camper may be removed from the truck bed with jacks — and work — thus freeing the truck of encumberances while you are zipping around the countryside.

While the same cannot be said of campers attached directly to the chassis, they are generally roomier and more solid.

You will find heavy duty tires worthwhile if you own a heavy camper, especially one which extends beyond the tailgate.

Some manufacturers make a unit which can be

raised for living and lowered for traveling, providing more stability with less wind resistance.

Also, truck campers have it over travel trailers in manoeuverability, both in town and in the boondocks.

Travel trailers come in sizes from 10 feet to more than 30 feet. The smallest size is suitable for little more than sleeping or eating, and lacks most "extras".

As the trailer grows, you will gain comfort and luxury with every foot.

Where do you house the beast when not in use? This can be a thorny problem for urbanites. Increasing numbers of devotees, not nomadic by nature, rent a lot by the year at a tent and trailer park, thus ridding themselves of storage headaches and the bother of battling traffic with trailer in tow. Off-season rates are usually minimal.

Today's deluxe models boast electric generators, heating plants, air conditioners, bath tubs and, even fold-out rooms—more amenities than most summer cottages.

Towing can be ticklish. Your car will have to be fitted with a frame hitch, and you will require the special load-levelling type if the tongue weight exceeds 150 pounds. That is the pressure your trailer exerts on the car hitch.

If you are improperly hitched or the load is not evenly distributed, you could be in for trouble in the form of "fish tailing". This is frightening for other highway travelers, and even scarier for you.

Fish tailing can become so violent that it can bounce the car completely out of control. On ice-covered or greasy highways it can trigger a violent skid which can only be stopped in the ditch, or in a pile-up with a post or another car.

If you are planning lengthy or numerous trailer outings, your car may require more doctoring than just the addition of mirrors and special hitches. An oversized alternator, large wheels and special tires should be considered. Give serious thought also to a transmission cooler, which is really a radiator circulating transmission fluid in the same manner your other radiator circulates water.

Backing up and parking are not easy. In this case practice will not make perfect, no matter how much you get, but you will become quite competent if you work at it. Parking lots which are abandoned on Sundays are good spots for practice sessions.

Just as you would not hit the trail without a spare automobile tire, you should never tow a trailer without toting a spare for it too. As the trailer tire is smaller and gets hotter, it is more likely to go "pow".

Motorhomes are growing in popularity, despite their astronomical price tag.

This is truly a mobile home, with all the comforts and luxuries of the most opulent trailer, plus the "no tow" feature.

Motorhomes are limited to highway travel, or graded secondary roads, and they are also limited to people with plenty of time and plenty of capital. They are ideal for people whose jobs keep them on the move, or for retired couples. It makes no sense for anyone to purchase one solely for an annual vacation.

Initial outlay plus maintenance, storage, insurance, depreciation and general operating costs preclude motorhomes becoming casual "sometime" vehicles.

Lack of back road mobility can be overcome by lashing bicycles or motor bikes to the exterior. And when you get weary, or traffic is horrendous, simply

pull to the side of the road and sleep, or wait it out.

For the average family, renting rather than buying a motor home makes sense.

Some motorhomes built in southern climates are not adequately insulated against cold weather. In frigid temperatures you will require a 20,000-30,000 B.T.U. gas heater, ducts, hot water and protection for water pipes to prevent freezing.

Camping on wheels can be a great adventure, providing more comfort than tent camping, plus the freedom to move quickly in the morning without wasting time breaking camp. And if campgrounds are full it is not a calamity.

Remember your manners; don't hold up traffic on hills. Pull to one side and let the gang pass you by. What's the hurry? Remember, you are having fun and it is your vacation.

CAMPING WITH CHILDREN

Kids take to camping like ducks to water. Tenting is a big adventure to small fry.

While their youthful enthusiasm and energy will have to be reined occasionally, it is usually contagious.

When are they old enough to bring along on a camping trip? Let's just say that they are really never too young. Even babes in arms can be indoctrinated. Always pack ample formula, food and diapers. And keep Baby well protected from sun, mosquitoes and flies. While Mom is saddled with the responsibility of caring for an infant, no vacation is a genuine holiday for her. But as she'll be quick to point out, it still beats staying at home.

When tenting with young children, unless you have a distant destination, don't be on the move every day.

Sit pat for a while. Relax. Give the youngsters a chance to make new friends and have some fun.

Besides, anyone with a family knows how hard a day's drive is for children.

"How many more miles dad?" "How long will it take us?" And, after fifteen minutes, "Is is two hours yet?"

The old standby of adding, subtracting and multiplying cows, windmills, cemeteries and white horses still help miles and minutes whiz by. Once in camp, there is no shortage of things to do.

To begin with, children will want to explore. Unless they are capable teenagers, don't turn them loose without a few territorial ground rules. These will depend upon your surroundings and vary each time you make a pitch.

But encourage them to make short sorties into the woods, where they can "stalk a bear"; and flee with wings on their heels if perchance they lay eyes on one. Teach them to identify poisonous plants, and to never eat berries until they have brought them back for the "all clear".

Insist that ranging kids wear a whistle on a lanyard. If they ever become confused as to direction, tell them to sit pat and give three shrill toots. Have a whistle yourself so that you can reply.

Many state and provincial parks boast nature trails where trees and other flora are identified with signs. Sometimes these skirt a beaver pond where, in the morning or evening, these industrious animals may be observed hard at work. Watch them from a downwind vantage point if possible. When they whack the water with their tails it's a signal that they have scented you and they will all retreat to the safety of their lodge.

Sometimes groups are led along these trails by park naturalists. Most park naturalists are interesting guides who are talking about things most dear to them, and have the correct answers to those incredible questions which curious kids come up with.

Sometimes there's a wildlife museum nearby, or a local scenic attraction well worth the side trip.

The evening is no problem. The best way for the family to spend it is around the campfire, roasting weiners, popping corn or toasting marshmallows.

When it's time to sack-out, it will be more pleasant for parents and more fun for youngsters if they have a shelter of their own, even if it is only a pup tent. They will have a ball. Be sure that they have a flashlight to check on noisy wild prowlers, and to use on their inevitable nightly safaris to the toilet.

Before leaving home, remind your youngsters to bring games, cards, reading material and colouring books to help pass the time during dreary, draggy downpours. This can be an opportune time for you to catch up on some of your own reading.

More than a day of that snail's pace will drive everyone bonkers, so if the inclemency continues either pack it up and move along, or head into the nearest town for the day.

One of the responsibilities of parenthood is seeing that your children learn how to swim. The campground is an ideal place to begin. If you happen to be a non-swimmer, some campgrounds offer instruction from experts. If so, you might enroll too. When they take a dip, always keep an eye on them, and never let them go swimming alone. The buddy system is imperative.

And fishing is a natural, whether at the campground or during a leg-stretching stop beside a river or lake.

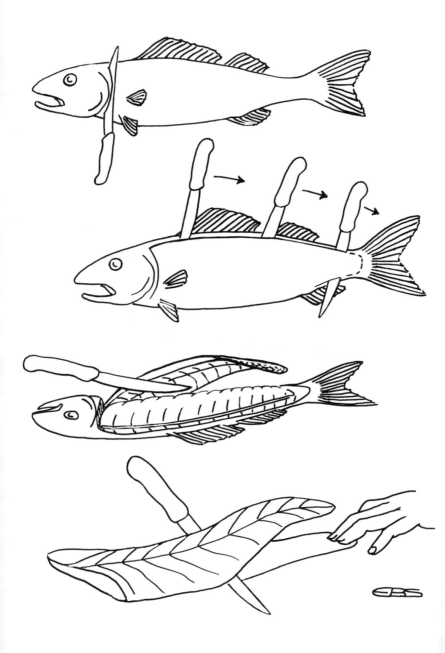

Youngsters don't give a hoot about the size or the species. All they crave is action. Docks and points of rock are generally productive for perch and panfish. And all that is needed is a hook and worm to entice the little scrappers into biting.

But buy your boy or girl their own rod and reels. Don't expect a child to cast with your cast-offs. It needn't be expensive and, if the child is small, one of the easily operated push-button models is best. Never, never let them fish or play near the water unless wearing a life jacket. You had better feature the catch on the dinner menu. Be prepared for a lengthy session with the cleaning knife.

One of my own favorite annual outings is a stag with my strapping teenage son, once school is out for the summer. He is big enough to portage the canoe, and still young enough to consider it fun.

Chapter Four

WILDERNESS CAMPING

CANOEING

Tenting on a tiny lot next to hundreds of other campers beats sweltering in a city apartment, but it is nonetheless rather akin to the situation you have just escaped.

It is like stopping on the threshold of Utopia, instead of taking those extra steps through the doorway. In sprawling crowded campgrounds, there is little chance to hear a loon, see a moose, catch a trout or, in some cases, even to bask in the reflection of a campfire.

The tranquility of solitude often awaits on the puffing side of a portage that is an hour away by paddle. A canoe can be a magic carpet to serenity seekers who abhor the madding crowd.

Those who have never paddled double-enders often fear them, and regard canoes as dangerous cockleshells. Some canoes are very tippy, but not the well-designed models. Also, stability increases with the confidence and competence of the paddler.

However, it is vitally important that canoeists be

good swimmers, or wear approved lifejackets at all times.

Paddling is a skill best learned between the gunwhales. No amount of descriptions or diagrams will teach as much as an expert will in a few minutes. After the first lesson, it becomes merely a question of perfection through practice.

I find it amazing that many people head out on a lake or down a river, usually in a rented canoe, without bothering to learn the basic principles of a simple J stroke.

I once had a ringside seat at the biggest display of ineptitude ever.

Two greenhorns were manipulating a canoe that the outfitter had left on a tiny wilderness lake. As they headed across the water, they sat facing each other; the man in the bow taking backstrokes with his paddle.

When the breeze swung the canoe about, as it did with regularity, their roles were also reversed.

As I recall, these gay blades struck out in the fishing game too.

Before tackling too ambitious a jaunt, rent a canoe and get the hang of it with some day trips. You will soon formulate logical opinions on the dimensions, materials, and other features which best suit your requirements.

Can there be that much difference in canoes? There certainly can be, and there is. Just as you would never purchase an automobile without a test drive, you should not buy a canoe without a test paddle.

I have been in some canoes which a sneeze would upset, some which paddled like scows, and others which rode the waters like balloons and were just about as easily controlled in a wind.

Unless you are a white water specialist, buy a canoe with a keel. Keel-less canoes are more difficult to keep on course. Also, there is nothing to protect their bottoms from boulders and other hazards lurking beneath the surface.

The broad, shallow shoe keel is a happy compromise between the standard type and no keel at all.

A square-stern canoe drags its tail, like a towboat. This type is designed for use with outboard motors, and is not intended for paddling, except in an emergency.

Not so with the V-stern model, which has only that portion of the stern which is out of the water squared off and reinforced to form a transom. The part beneath the surface still slices water as it should.

In many respects V-stern models are ideal if you intend to be motor-powered. You will have no motor bracket to bother about. These brackets clamp onto the canoe and project out of the side, slightly back of the stern seat.

While it is said that operating an outboard motor on a V-stern is awkward because the controls are behind you, I have never found this to be a drawback in the many years that I have owned and operated one.

It is a more stable arrangement than a side bracket, because the motor is dead centre.

Why use an outboard on a canoe? Doesn't it noisily defeat the purpose of the exercise?

That depends. The one and two horsepower engines are almost as quiet as the battery-powered electric motors. Unfortunately, battery-powered electric motors are not suited for out-tripping. Batteries are brutes to portage, and there are no outlets in the wilds where they can be rejuvenated.

A tiny gas-operated outboard will putt-putt all day on a pint or two of fuel, and it weighs so little that it is easy to portage.

The maximum pleasures of canoeing do come with a dipping paddle. And you will never pare your bulging waistline by letting a motor do the work, but for some types of fishing, especially trolling, a motor is essential.

When dragging a lure over snag-filled waters, it can become very wearisome to backpaddle fifty yards for each 150 yards of progress, especially when a stiff breeze is blowing.

Since the windward shore is the one most anglers head toward, because that is where fishing is best, motors are almost as vital as rods and reels. But for river travel, motors are more of a hindrance than a help.

Incidentally, a crafty stern man will outfish the bow man every time. After passing a promising pool or riffle, nose the bow well into the alders or bushes, and the stern is then ideally positioned for a productive cast.

The traditional canoe, except the birchbark canoe is the canvas-covered wooden craft. These canoes still make up a big piece of the market which they have had cornered for well over a century.

While the well-designed canvas and wood double-enders are comfortable for travel, even the lightest canoes are fairly heavy. And they get heavier. It has been estimated that they absorb up to fifteen pounds of water. More weight is added each time they're painted.

Nowadays some makers are covering their craft with verolite, a vinyl-impregnated fabric reputed to be lighter than the conventional canvas skin, boasting twice the scuff-resistance and never requiring painting.

Fiberglass canoes have come a long way in a few years. Some featherweight models are almost paper-thin, yet strong enough to withstand a pounding by a hammer.

Many people who scoffed at aluminum canoes when they first appeared, are now paddling one themselves. No, they do not become hot, as some who have never been inside one seem to think. In fact, if anything, they can be too cold at times.

The stretch-formed aluminum craft are tough. They can be battered and banged, yet never leak a drop. And they are maintenance free. Turn them over and forget about them until you are heading out again. Neither rain, nor sleet, nor snow...etc.

Exceptions are the ultra-light metal canoes lined with ethafoam, many of which are painted to simulate birchbark.

Few of them are tough enough to take the punishment of a rough river run, but they are ideal for small lakes. They are so light that even a child can tote one across a portage.

Being extremely short (twelve feet) and beamy (three feet), and having stabilizing sponsons outside the gunwales, ethafoam canoes can be awkward to paddle, particularly in a wind. But they row really well, and most are equipped with oarlocks and paddles which have pins attached for instant conversion.

The most eye-appealing canoe in my books, is made from half-lap strips of British Columbia cedar. It is light as a feather and, with the addition of a protective coat of clear fiberglass, will take the knocks too.

It's important to pack the canoe in such a way that the load is evenly distributed for level riding.

If a third person is along, make certain that he sit on the bottom. For extra stability the paddlers should rest on their knees, with their rear ends partially supported by the canoe's seats.

When alone, you will probably find that the canoe handles best when you paddle from the bow seat, facing stern. This sometimes precludes the need for a boulder ballast.

When heading into a wind, try to set your course so you can expend your energies on paddling, not steering.

A pair of canoes can be lashed together so that they will safely negotiate rough seas.

Lash them four feet apart at their bows and six feet at their sterns with strong green poles. If traveling downwind, rig a makeshift sail and you will virtually fly across the waves.

Portaging can be a mean chore for those who have toted needless paraphernalia. It is those extra round trips which tire you. Keep in mind that a canoe carries more comfortably with one person underneath it. Also remember that it gains pounds as you gain years.

Most yokes which come with canoes are badly designed, and will dig into your neck or shoulders on a long haul. A yoke should distribute the weight across back, neck and shoulders. To do this well, it must be "tailored" to you. Just as another guy's suit will rarely fit you, neither will a "standard" yoke.

Most canoeists slip the paddles under ropes looped on the thwarts, and let the blades rest on their shoulders during the lift. It is a good idea to drape a rolled towel, sweater or shirt around your neck to cushion the thwart. Take the sleeves of the shirt or sweater, bring them around under your arms, and tie or button them behind your back.

If you are toting a framed rucksack, you will discover that when the thwart is resting on it, you will have distributed the weight of the craft so that it is even easier to carry.

In lieu of lifting, the lining technique is often favored on rivers. This is done by attaching ropes — at least fifty feet in length — to bow and stern. It can best be manipulated with one person on each end, although an individual can handle the job by tying the two ends together.

While most paddles are spruce or cedar, ash or maple is tougher and less likely to split. Drill a hole through the grip so that it can be hung on a nail at home or out of harm's way in camp. The paddles' length depends on your own agility, preference and physique. Somewhere from chin to forehead height is the normal length.

When pushing off shore or away from rocks with a paddle, reverse it and shove with the blade in your hand.

A pole in the hands of an adept sternman is the way to run shallow rivers. These poles are usually ten or more feet in length and, if you buy one for the job, it will come equipped with a metal cap or shoe. It is a good tool for holding a canoe in position and fending through crash courses.

Always have a third paddle lashed inside the craft to press into service in the event of breakage or loss.

Running a river is a good way to tear or puncture a canoe. Canvas-covered models can be repaired by smearing cement under the gash, adding the patch, covering it with glue, then pressing the outside skin together again. An outside patch will serve in an emergency, and if you lack cement, use tree resin. Some tapes are strong and watertight. I completed a trip with masking tape covering two cuts, and it held.

Shooting fast water is tricky, but fun. Look the run over carefully on foot first, and either lash your gear inside or carry it on *terra firma.*

Rivers are the roads of the wilderness, with new scenes and surprises awaiting around each bend.

Plan well ahead so that you can make a circle route. It's no fun battling the current back upstream. Study maps, but don't rely on them one hundred percent. I will never forget one jaunt which the map indicated had twelve sets of rapids and falls. We traversed a total of sixty-five! The topographers must have photographed the river from the air during high water.

An 86-page U.S. booklet "Maikens Guide to U.S. Canoe Trails" is available from Le Voyageur Publishing Co., 1318 Wentwood Drive, Irving, Texas 75061.

"Plan now, paddle later" is advice from Nick Nickels, Lakefield, Ontario K0L 2H0, author of "Canada Canoe Routes"—150 pages chock-full of information about canoe tripping from British Columbia to Newfoundland.

HIKING AND BACKPACKING

I gingerly dabbed alcohol on my sore, blistered feet. I had a raw spot on one hip where the frame of my rucksack had rubbed after rivets fastening the shoulder strap had popped out. My breeches hung limply; it did not take long for stomach muscles to pull together again.

This was the result of spending several days marching with the bunion brigade. Never again? Not at all.

In fact, I had promised myself to do this more often, and was already looking forward to my next trek.

Autumn is my favorite time to give shank's mare a workout, and during these three days on the trail the foliage was ablaze, the bugs had left the scene, and we did not meet another soul.

Due to today's "getting back to nature" exodus, hiking has become a major factor in putting the populace back on its feet.

Almost daily, new trails are being opened, and existing ones are being lengthened and improved. The famous Appalachian Trail in the eastern United States, and the Bruce Trail in central Ontario are among the most heavily traveled.

Someday soon the continent will be veined with linking hiking paths from coast to coast, and from Mexico to northern Canada.

Much credit for clearing, marking and mapping these routes goes to many dedicated clubs and associations. Their tireless devotion is responsible for the burgeoning number of trails, and they often struggle and plead with governments and individual landowners every foot of the way.

Heading for the hills for days at a stretch with your camp on your back is a far cry from a Sunday afternoon stroll through the park.

The most important equipment is your footwear. Ideally, they will be proper six-inch hiking boots with a flexible lug or vibram sole. The uppers will be leather and have padded ankles and elasticized tops. Hook lacing is another good feature.

Many of the ankle-high and ten-inch hunting boots

are fine for trekking. Steer clear of sneakers, mocassins, sandals, leather-soled "street shoes", rubber boots, nearly-inflexible mountaineering boots, and other unsuitable footwear.

However, the comfort of mocassins is welcome after a day on the trail. A second pair of walking boots are useful to have if the boots you are wearing get soaked or ruined.

Always break in new footwear before it is called on for combat duty. Wear it to the office or shop, for constitutionals, for lawn mowing, etc. But do not make its first test the crucial one.

You will probably develop blisters, regardless. This condition is hastened and worsened if socks are damp. Always carry spare clean socks, even if you are out only for the day.

I wear two pairs of woollen socks, even in warm weather. They absorb perspiration and cushion the feet. Sprinkling with talcum powder also helps keep socks dry.

If I am walking cleared and established trails, I like the freedom and comfort of shorts or breeches worn with woollen knee socks. Switch to trousers if your route is laced with burrs, brambles, bush and thorns, or when bugs are about. A mosquito will ram her rapier through the socks, and a black fly will burrow between the stitches.

Mesh underwear is perfect for backpackers, because it encourages evaporation of perspiration instead of it being soaked into your clothing. Don't be startled by the net appearance of the skin on your shoulders after a day toting a pack. Fear not, you are not disfigured for life.

Don't be a blister-buster. That is dangerous. Cover

the blister with a band-aid to prevent additional irritation and limp along. If your boots fit, after a few outings your feet will toughen to the game and blisters will be rare.

With the proper pack, today's lightweight fabrics and freeze-dried or dehydrated foods, there is no need to travel laden like a packhorse. Nor is a spartan bivouac necessary.

Included in my pack are such basics for a comfortable camp as mattress, sleeping bag, fly sheet, and tent — all of which total eleven pounds!

I also bring along a rainsuit, a candle lantern, a mess kit, food, a pack rod, reel and tackle, a flashlight, a saw, a first aid kit, a camera and lenses, a wee drop, a change of clothing, spare boots, etc.

The items and weight fluctuate with the length of the hike, terrain, weather, proximity to civilization, etc. I don't have to lay the load on a scale to know when it exceeds the thirty-pound limit prescribed by many backpackers.

But by heck, even an old-style feminine female can carry that much. I reckon that if a man can't trot all day with half a hundred pounds, he shouldn't tackle overnight hikes in the first place.

It is important to have your gear properly packed. A full pack can appear impressive without its weight being oppressive.

Even more important than the pack is the frame to which it is attached. Ensure the pack frame's construction passes your stringent inspection. A broken strap, a popped rivet, a twisted frame, can make what is left of a pleasant jaunt an arduous trek.

If the frame does not come with padded shoulder straps, buy straps which slip or snap on. It should have a padded hip belt, and fit comfortably without any of the metal tubing touching your back. If the one you see first does not fill the bill, then keep looking. Pack frames come in different lengths, so get one which is right for you.

We have used frames on deer hunts to tote a white-tail carcass back to camp. One man can puff home with as much as 200 pounds of venison on his shoulders, and an average 135 pounder is a cinch.

The majority of packs designed to fit these frames are yellow, red or orange nylon. This material and these colors are first rate.

The pack should have separate horizontal zippered compartments, small pockets on the ends, strap holders for fishing rod tubes, and an outside map pouch.

While packframes have muscled the metal-framed European rucksacks out of the limelight, European rucksacks are still excellent and are appreciated by all who have ever worn one.

Mine have been strong, faithful companions for more than two decades of wilderness travel. They are cool too, if made so the heavy webbed band which goes across the small of the back keeps the frame and packs away from your body.

The pack basket is a long-time favorite of campers and hikers in the northeastern United States. It is lightweight, yet very strong, and its rigid construction makes it a perfect container for food, cameras and other breakables or crushables.

Another which still enjoys widespread use is the big, undivided packsack of twelve to sixteen ounce watertight duck, boasting tumpline and thick leather shoulder straps. It is sometimes called the Duluth.

Don't use it for hiking, but it is great for canoeing. With the aid of the tumpline, a sturdy neck and a sloping stature, it can be used to haul heavy loads for long distances.

As I have mentioned before, how you load is a key factor in comfort and energy output. Keep sharp objects away from the back of the pack. Stow the lightest gear in the bottom and keep the heaviest items on top.

A belt pouch, such as worn by skiers, is useful for hikers to stash matches, compass, pipes, billfold, tobacco, etc.

Hiking is a great family activity, and the toddler who accompanies his folks safely ensconsed in a "papoose" baby carrier will be as happy as a sandman. Have you ever seen an Indian baby on a "cradle board" crying? Neither have I.

However, indoctrinate slowly.

Two families can band together to explore a leg of a trail, and by parking a car at either end, they will not have to retrace their steps.

Hiking is a dandy one-day diversion from campground life. Once hardened physically and steeped in experience, you may wish to get off the beaten track, practice independence and see new sights. But always take your time. Listen and observe. Hike for the joy, the exercise, the experience. And when you hobble into the daylight, the morning after your first day on the trail, you may be footsore, but you'll also be fancy free!

Chapter Five

SNOW CAMPING

A WHITE WORLD AWAITS

Winter campers can be roughly divided into two categories—the happy and the hapless. The one-shot "never again!" gang probably failed the test of cold weather tenting because they didn't do their homework and bone-up on snow know-how.

Proper planning is always a requisite, but it gains importance when you make your pitch in the snow. In howling winds and sub-zero temperatures, the smallest item of gear is vital to comfort and well-being.

Snow camping can be just as pleasant as the summertime version; actually even more so, because all the bugs are hibernating.

But it can also be hellish, as I discovered on my first such camp-out during the Ice Age, sometime between the last dinosaur and the first snowmobile! Time has failed to thaw the chilly memories of that ill-fated outing, which proved a testimonial to the adage that experience is the best teacher.

With the impetuousness of youth, we had ignored a cardinal camping rule by not even making a check list. There wasn't time. Acting on a spur-of-the-moment whim, we packed and were on our way within minutes.

We had dressed too warmly for the strenuous snowmobile trek through the woods to the lake, and were wringing with perspiration when we arrived. Needless to say, we were soon chilled to the marrow.

Our ignorance compounded our discomfort when we erected the canvas on the lake's frozen surface, so that the fishing would be literally on our doorstep. That logic applies to an ice-fishing hut, but not to a tent.

Even a roaring reflector fire failed to chase the chills from those exposed diggings, and hefty stringers of walleyes did little to compensate for the physical miseries of that weekend. We both developed colossal colds as hacking reminders of our ineptness.

That was my first and last snowtime junket which called for reserves of intestinal fortitude. Armed with knowledge and common sense, all my subsequent excursions have been comfortable.

A common complaint of the neophyte is "I was so busy surviving I didn't have time to enjoy myself." That would not happen if people would learn to work with winter instead of fighting it.

The tranquility of the winter camper's surroundings cannot be matched during any other season. In the white woods he can rest in peace without a slab of granite on his head. A sandwich tastes like a gourmet meal, a jug of java tops vintage wine, and a pipe has never puffed sweeter.

There, where winter's white blanket has hushed the hubbub, and the only sounds are those of silence, you can easily come to terms with yourself and with life.

If the snow camper also happens to be a shutterbug, he will find that he is in Utopia. Snowscapes, highlighted with sunshine and contrasted with shadow, offer endless photographic challenges.

And when the trees are void of foliage and the ground has changed from brown to white, the opportunities to capture wildlife on film are greatly multiplied. Many animals are loathe to move off through deep snow unless threatened with a very real danger, and they frequently appear to sense that the nature photographer means them no harm. Birds and animals seem to shed some of their inherent wariness in the winter months.

There are certain pitfalls in winter photography which one must guard against. Shutters may freeze or become sluggish, and incorrect exposures are frequently caused by failing to compensate for the brilliant reflection of sunlight off the snow.

The best advice is "have your camera winterized". This is an expensive process involving the removal of all the oil and grease, replacing it with graphite or other sub-zero lubricants.

The cheapest alternative is to keep your camera under your coat between shots. Avoid overheating it, or you will be in for condensation problems. Kodak suggests using covers of black felt or fur because they afford protection from the icy blasts and absorb some of the sun's heat.

Ice-fishing can provide a pleasant and often exciting diversion for the winter camper. In fact, that is the main reason angling enthusiasts are under canvas.

The most basic equipment will usually suffice, and all the tackle you will need can be carried in your pocket. A short jigging rod, a tip-up or a tilt are all acceptable.

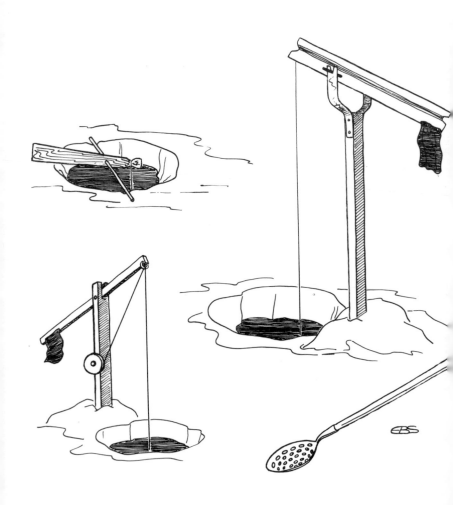

Add a spool of monofilament line, a couple of jigging lures or some minnows, a spreader, and you are in business after you have cut a hole in the ice. The chisels and augers designed for the job are both satisfactory. Axes are not.

Certain species of fish and some lakes and rivers are closed to winter angling, so always check local fishing regulations before you wet a line. One plus for ice-fishing is that you do not have to worry about your catch spoiling in the heat.

Those who enjoy rabbit hunting will rarely need to venture far from camp to get a bunny in their sights. The most common species is the varying hare, called "snowshoes" because of its huge feet. Being the same color as the snow, it can be tricky to spot. The best places to look for hares are low-lying areas such as cedar swamps, or in reforestation woodlots, especially places where the lower branches are not trimmed.

Rabbit stew is delicious, be it eaten in the dining room or while perched beside a blazing campfire.

There are many energetic pastimes for the camper. The three favorites — snowshoeing, snowmobiling and cross-country skiing — will be discussed in detail in subsequent chapters.

Snow camping can, and should be, a great, invigorating adventure. However, it should be tackled initially with a degree of caution, especially if it is going to involve the whole family.

The tyro should try his hand in one of the state or provincial parks where winter camping is encouraged. Many boast such amenities as heated toilets, hot water, electrical outlets, ploughed campsites and free firewood. And, what may just prove to be the best deal of all, you can park your car where it will be handy for a fast getaway!

BEATING THE BRRRS

If you equip, dress, and camp correctly, your snowy sojourn will not become a freezefest. Begin by selecting a site protected from prevailing winds, and dig away the snow to a depth of six inches. A snowshoe doubles as a shovel for this job. Do not make the mistake of pitching on bare, frozen ground when it can be avoided; without the insulating snow it can be like bedding down on a slab of ice. I generally double the insulation by heaping half a foot of spruce boughs on the snow before erecting my canvas.

Because heat is precious and hard to come by, do not make a shelter larger than dictated by your basic requirements. Great for winter camping is a pair of identically shaped tents, one slightly larger than the other. By pitching the small unit inside the larger unit, you will have two thicknesses of fabric to break the wind and an insulating dead air space between them. Of course, the mountaineering tents with tunnel entrances and sleeve ventilators are ideal protection, but are inclined to be rather cramped. Lacking such specialized gear, a flysheet will serve as a wind break and keep your tent dry.

Pegs are next to useless when the soil is frozen solid. That is when a tent with outside sodcloth is ideal, as it can be weighted with logs around its perimeter.

Having anchored the tent, bank snow around its base and your den will be as snug as a hibernating bear's.

While on a ptarmigan hunt along the bleak frozen tundra of James Bay, we had no choice but to camp out, there being no hostelries along that isolated coastline.

The tent—a commodious eight foot by twelve foot

job used to house autumn goose shooters — was standing in a thicket of willows and stunted poplars which afforded little protection from the bone-chilling northers.

Heat was supplied by an oil-drum wood stove which devoured the poplar fuel as quickly as it was fed.

While the mercury plummeted to fifty degrees below zero at night, we slept cosily. The walls had been banked to the pitch of the roof, and we were snugly ensconced below snow level.

Catalytic tent heaters are the answer for the average winter camper. If fuel is not rationed, it is a good idea to let it glow away all day in order to keep chills and condensation at bay.

Cat heaters burn naphtha fumes and are safe and explosion-proof, as are the alcohol burning heaters, which are extremely effective but costly to operate.

Unfortunately, many catalytic heaters do not radiate sufficient heat to keep a dog house warm. You would be well-advised to buy one of the 5000 b.t.u. models, and under no circumstances go for anything less than 3500 b.t.u.'s.

Lanterns and camp stoves are also excellent heaters, although, for safety's sake, the latter are not recommended for indoor use. When using any of these oxygen-gulping appliances, ensure that there is ample ventilation. Never ignite them inside, and always extinguish them before you call it a day.

There is no place on the snow camping check-list for camp cots. Air mattresses are fairly satisfactory, but the best are made of polyether foam. They offer warmth and comfort, in addition to fighting condensation by "breathing".

There's no arguing a sleeping bag isn't a top priority item either. Nor should you kid yourself into believing your summer-weight bag will be warm enough. It won't be.

Two of them, one inside the other, might do the job. So might one lightweight robe, after inserting one or two wool blankets.

Naturally, the down-filled sleeping bags designed for Arctic climates are the most satisfactory. Many boast a wool liner or an inner bag, and are filled with at least five pounds of down. A baffled zipper is a feature to look for, as is walled construction which eliminates the cold spots along the stitching.

While the mummy-style is warmest, avoid them like the plague if you are as claustrophobic as I am.

I once purchased one before heading into the wilds, reasoning that it would be just fine since it combined cosiness with compactness. We were holed up in a trapper's line shanty. It had been an exhausting day and minutes after squeezing into my down-filled tube, I was dead to the world.

Some time during the night I awoke to find myself twisted inside that cocoon in such a way that my face was buried and my arms pressed so tightly against my body that I was unable to move them to find the escape hatch. Naturally I panicked.

With a heave of arms and shoulders, I split my straight-jacket from top to bottom and broke free of its constrictor-like embrace. So many feathers filled the air that the crude shanty resembled a chicken-plucking plant!

Buy a bag that is large enough to allow you to comfortably submerge in it. A heavy six-foot man should no more purchase a standard size sleeping robe than buy a hat several sizes too small for his head.

If your companion is the little woman, in the interests of warmth and togetherness, zip your bags together to form a double-bed model. However, they must be identical in order to join properly.

Wool or insulated longjohns make excellent pyjamas, provided that you haven't been running around in them all day. Wear wool socks too, and, if your head gets cold, don a balaclava nightcap.

Condensation and perspiration are the two biggest enemies of the winter camper. It is vital that your bed be kept moisture-free. Turn your sleeping bag inside-out each day and dry it thoroughly. Check your mattress too, since you may discover it is damp on top.

By understanding why you get cold, you can utilize that knowledge to your advantage.

Conduction is a major chilling factor, and it commonly takes place through the soles of the feet. It also occurs when frozen objects are touched with bare hands, or when sitting or lying on cold ground.

It's true that a warm hat can curb cold feet. When your head and torso are warm, the surface blood vessels transmit the excess body heat to your fingers and toes, which act as radiators. A parka hood is superior to a hat or cap, as it minimizes heat loss through the neck.

Insulated leather boots are good footwear. They breathe to some extent, keeping condensation minimal. However, when they do get wet, drying them in camp is a lengthy chore.

While snowmobile boots with felt liners do not offer much ankle support, they are A-1 in the warmth category. Always take an extra pair of liners on an overnight excursion. Felt soaks up moisture and is slow to dry.

Ensure that your boots are big enough to accommodate insoles and a couple of pairs of wool socks. Felt or goat's hair insoles are best and, in the sock department, wool wins feet down. Wool has the unique characteristic of providing some warmth even when wet.

Do not venture too far afield without spare socks and insoles. The best place to carry these is not in your pack, but next to your body where they will stay warm and dry.

Mittens lack the dexterity of gloves but are much warmer. If you intend to handle cold equipment, such as cameras and guns, try wearing silk gloves inside the mittens. Join your mittens as kids do, with a cord running inside your sleeves; then you cannot lose them, and when you take one off, you needn't hang onto it with the other hand.

You may have noticed that people living or working in the far north frequently wear duffle-cloth mittens inside leather mittens. That is a hot combination. Many also award a gold star to socks of the same material.

Snowmobile suits are great for the purpose for which they were designed, or for such pastimes as ice-fishing. However, they are portable steam cabinets when worn for snowshoeing, skiing, or other activities involving physical exertion.

The human body generates one and a half pints of moisture every 12 hours, so any gain over condensation is a victory for comfort.

Shun apparel which cuts off circulation, such as elastics on ski pants, snug belts and tight boots.

In fact, there is a plank in the women's lib platform with which I agree. Women should certainly doff their tight-fitting "unmentionables", at least when on sub-zero sojourns.

Wear long underwear that is designed to trap air next to your body. The waffle-weave types are good, but the best by far are the mesh or "fishnet" longjohns.

A secret for happy outdoors living in winter is to dress in layers of clothing which can be taken off during strenuous activity and put on again when resting.

One of my favorite garments is a down vest which keeps my torso snug and my arms free. It can be rolled and stuffed into the outside pocket of my pack.

A handwarmer is a welcome gadget after you have had your hands exposed while fiddling with cameras or rigging fishing lines. I personally prefer the type which burns solid fuel. These virtually refuse to go out on their own, whereas I have had running battles to keep others lit.

With a little knowledge and forethought, there is no need to be among winter camping's cooler customers.

SNOWSHOEING

For experienced winter campers, getting there is half the fun. For ill-prepared neophytes, it is half the battle.

The vehicles generally used to span the gap between the weekday pace and weekend peace are snowshoes, skis and snowmobiles.

Even in this age of motorized toboggans, snowshoe sales still plod along at a steady pace. And while the tortoise will never overtake the hare in dollar volume, he does threaten to pass him in unit volume.

In fact, the snowmobile has given the snowshoe industry a boost. Prudent snowmobilers never leave the beaten track without snowshoes lashed to their machines, and snowmobiling has introduced thousands of raw recruits to the outdoors, many of whom now seek new horizons on the webs.

The wide range of sizes and styles can spell confusion to the tyro. It is very important to choose shoes best-suited to your measurements and requirements. If they are too small, you will wallow to your knees in the white stuff, and if they are too large you will trip over your own webbed feet.

Flat toes are a feature of some models, including the "lumberman", "beavertail" and some "bear paw". They are useful when climbing packed or icy slopes, but are no great help in deep snow.

Long slim snowshoes are best when traveling across open country, such as lakes and fields. These average twelve inches in width, and five feet in length. Their labels include "Ojibway", "U.S. Army" and "Cross-Country".

Many trappers and hare hunters give the nod to a tail-less shoe, mostly because it is manoeuverable in dense bush and can be negotiated over deadfalls with little effort. The most popular is the 14-inch x 30-inch curved-toe "bear paw", followed by the 10-inch x 36-inch "otter".

The track left by a greenhorn trekking on a pair of these platters will resemble a drunken sailor's.

Why is there a tail on snowshoes? It does help keep you afloat by absorbing a few of your pounds-per-square-inch, but its main function is to help to steer a straight course.

The best all-round snowshoes for the camping crowd have turned-up toes and tails.

The 14-inch x 42-inch model will prove ideal for the average man who weighs between 140 pounds and 175 pounds. Women can more easily manipulate a shoe one or two inches narrower, while men in the heavyweight category will need webs which are at least 14-inches x 48-inches. A range of kids' shoes is available, including some which measure 9-inches x 29-inches. These are perfect for the small fry.

Most snowshoes are framed with white ash, just as they have been for centuries. Some of the newest models employ magnesium, which is lighter in weight than wood, but comes with a heavier price tag.

Be wary of the small plastic models often sold to snowmobilers as "survival" equipment. Large numbers made in the Far East are of questionable quality, and too small to support anyone except a child.

The "gut" lacing nowadays is actually cowhide; whereas the Indians used caribou, moose or deer skin.

Choose shoes laced with thick leather from the animal's back. These stay taut, and are often guaranteed not to sag. Snowshoes strung with thinner leather from the lower flanks often "belly" when wet, or after prolonged use.

Don't skimp when selecting a harness. It is frequently the weak link which breaks the chain of happy hours in the outdoors.

The harness should be made from thick, oiled leather, and be fitted with heavy straps, large rivets, durable buckles and strong lacing.

When securing the harness to the snowshoe with thongs, soak the leather in water before you begin the job. It will stretch while being secured and will be extra tight when dry.

A broken strap can be a near-emergency if you are miles from home. I always carry a repair kit consisting of thongs, knife and a leather punch.

Some safety-conscious snowshoers make a harness which has a rubber toe cap and no heel strap. Then, should you break through the ice on a pond, lake or river, the snowshoes can be easily kicked off.

I must admit I don't use them, although there was a day when I regretted not using them. I was tracking two moose which had circled a beaver pond. Thinking I would save myself some steps, I web-footed across, intending to pick up their trail again on the other side. Although we had had bitterly cold weather and it was then January, the pond had not safely frozen, possibly due to beaver activity. As I reached the center of the pond the ice gave way and I was into the swim.

No, I did not drown, but I could have. My feet were still tied to my four-foot snowshoes, and I can assure you that it is no cinch unbuckling them underwater in mid-winter!

Despite this traumatic experience, I still have leather bindings, but I am much more cautious when crossing ice.

Some old-timers fashion their harness from tough, inexpensive lampwick. However, these harnesses are not as convenient or as comfortable as the conventional type.

If properly cared for, quality snowshoes will last for many years. Maintenance entails an annual coat of varnish, and storage in a cool, dry place in the off-season.

The felt-lined, flat-soled snowmobiling boots are very good for snowshoeing. Mukluks or high moccasins are even better, being lighter and giving more support.

You will discover that long ski poles are a big help when you climb hills or clamber over obstacles, especially when you are weighted down with a heavily laden pack.

Try to fit your camp on your back, with the aid of a pack frame.

If you have more than you can pile between your shoulder blades, you will probably have to haul a sled or toboggan. A toboggan is the better choice, because it is less likely to become mired and is effortlessly towed. Towing is best done with the help of a chest or shoulder strap.

While you may have to make do with the type of toboggan kids use, the best style for towing a load is tapered and much narrower.

Do not be too ambitious the first few days you are on snowshoes. You will discover aches where you did not even know you had places. Snowshoeing is not considered a strenuous activity, but when the going is heavy and the terrain is varied, you will give your body a stiffer workout than it is accustomed to. You will use leg muscles which are rarely pressed into service.

I learned this the hard way. After a six-hour hike during the first snowfall of the season, I was bitten by a charley horse, which didn't let go for several minutes, leaving me with some very sore and colourful thigh muscles.

To conclude, snowshoes provide inexpensive mobility for the snow camper seeking adventure in the wild white yonder.

SKIING

Cross-country skiing has been a Rip Van Winkle.

It is no new arrival. In fact, it has been about for thousands of years, but because it did not make any snowmobile sounds, few took any notice.

It is a great way to go. It is swift, silent, and an excellent physical conditioner.

Ski jumpers get oohs and aahs as they soar like birds. It is exciting to watch, but hardly the pastime to tackle when a jog around the block assumes formidable proportions.

And the Alpine branch of the sport does not fit most family budgets. Also, the swingles and après ski activities featured in beer advertisements don't exactly attract the family man.

Jammed slopes and long tow line-ups turn many off too.

Then suddenly, the get-away-from-it-all-and-return-to-nature movement discovered cross country skiing, which is more appropriately labelled ski touring.

It is ideal for the snow camper, and fits the "family fun" category to a "t".

So, from a handful of hard-core devotees a few years ago, participation has mushroomed until now tens of thousands are into the game.

Check the cost of outfitting the family and you will get a pleasant surprise. The outlay is amazingly low. In fact, it is possible to buy a satisfactory outfit for as little as $50, and $75 will purchase excellent quality boots, poles, skis and harness.

There is more to selecting the equipment than meets the eye. Seek the advice of an expert, or discover a ski shop with salesmen who are ski-touring specialists.

Do some reading on the subject before you invest in what might be an unwise choice. I recommend that you read Ned Baldwin's *The Cross Country Skiing Handbook*. Baldwin is an off-the-beaten-track specialist, and his suggestions are sound for the snow-camping crowd.

Buy touring skis, or those called "light touring". The touring skis are the widest, up to seventy millimetres, and the light touring range up to fifty-six millimetres. Steer clear of the narrow ultra-light racing runners which average about forty-eight millimetres in width. It goes without saying, heavyweights require stiffer skis than those of smaller proportions.

The bindings are quite basic, with the simple toe binding being the most popular. Simple toe bindings are fine for trail, field and lake travel, but when tackling more challenging terrain, a cable harness is more suitable. It is important to get the harness properly mounted so that the toe of your boot will be over the ski's balance point.

You will find little similarity between the rigid boots worn by Alpine skiers and the flexible footwear of touring buffs.

Cross country boots are light, and resemble soccer boots at first glance. The highest style, padded around the top is the warmest, and will keep the most snow out. A composition sole of polyurethane is advisable. Keep the uppers waterproof and steer clear of moisture-soaking suede. Plan to wear anklets or knee-high gaiters in deep snows or on extended outings. Wet legs and feet are uncomfortable and can be dangerous.

If you stand outside for a few moments before taking off, the boots have an opportunity to cool. They will then be less likely to get wet because of snow melting on them.

Waxing is a tricky business. Not only in its application, but in the selection of the correct wax for the current snow conditions.

When scaling slopes, the right wax coupled with expert application will help you avoid sliding backwards. Carry at least three different waxes so that you will be prepared for whatever snow conditions you encounter en route or in camp.

You can climb some hills straight up, others by a sidestep or by a herringbone technique. In some cases, you will be forced to remove the skis and make it on foot.

Practice for your wilderness test in a park or on a golf course. Few golf courses permit snowmobiling, but most have no objection to skiers using the snow-blanketed fairways.

You cannot do without poles. Fiberglass shafts are the strongest, but shafts made from tonkin are lighter and less expensive. Unlike the cross-country racer, the ski tourer needs poles with large baskets to lend additional support and give more push in deep snows.

Sunglasses should be worn to cut the glare from brilliant sunshine on snow, to shield your eyes from biting winds and to preclude the chance of snow blindness. Some skiers wear the non-fogging goggles used by snowmobilers and Alpine skiers.

Do not overdress; a mistake neophytes are prone to make. Ski touring is reasonably strenuous exercise, and while you are on the go, even in cold weather, your body generates heat.

Wear layers of lightweight clothing, which may be easily peeled as you warm up.

Since Baldwin recommends a headband instead of a toque or balaclava, we can assume his head is still thatched. But if your scalp has grown through your hair, you will need a substitute.

What about the knickers so often seen on ski tourers? They are more than a uniform. They permit freedom of movement, thus enabling you to glide along smoothly and rhythmically.

When skiing to your campsite, it is necessary to tote your camp on your back. This is accomplished with the help of a packframe.

Ski touring will leave you stiff and sore until you are accustomed to the exercise. Tackle day trips for starters. On these, you can eliminate most gear except a jacket, extra socks, and the ingredients for a lunch.

Do not strike out on your own, unless absolutely necessary. If you do, let someone know your destination, probable route, and anticipated return time.

SNOWMOBILING

Nobody has a "no comment" on the subject of snowmobiles.

People love them or hate them. In truth, the beast is neither black nor white, but pale grey.

Snowmobiles are certainly a boon to the snow camping fraternity. Helped by the snowmobile, campers can reach wonderful scenic settings which would otherwise have remained inaccessible. This willing workhorse will tow a sled full of family or gear without complaining, thus enabling you to bring along kids or amenities which would never fit in a rucksack.

Around the campsite it can be harnessed to haul logs, firewood and water. In fact, I would still be packing moosemeat if it were not for the 10 horse power snowmobile with which I skidded the whole carcass for many miles out of the remote wilderness and back to civilization.

If the latent gypsy in your soul finds a mobile camping adventure appealing, simply hitch onto one of the tent-campers on skis, and away you go. Most look disturbingly like coffins when folded for travel, but in little more time than it takes to pop open an umbrella, they will bloom into cosy shelters. Most feature two benches, a table, a window, a door and a couple of trap doors on the floor; the trap doors can be opened when you are parked over an ice-fishing hole.

I have found them satisfactory as fishing huts, and very good as mid-day lunchrooms. But they are no great shakes as overnight shelters in bitterly cold weather. The only way to make them comfortable then is to virtually bury them in the snow.

"Never go it alone" is the most important safety rule when venturing off the beaten track. As with swimming, the buddy system is a requisite. There are a number of hazards against which the snowmobile-camper must guard. Drowning is high on the list, and many devotees enter a watery grave each winter. Check ice conditions carefully before crossing lakes. Currents in rivers make ice conditions especially hazardous. At least seven inches of clear blue ice is needed for worry-free snowmobiling.

If you are zipping along at a moderate twenty miles per hour in zero degree weather, you are facing a mind-boggling wind chill factor of thirty-nine degrees below zero. Any exposed anatomy can freeze in minutes; so always make sure that you are well muffled.

Goggles are necessary to protect eyes from biting winds and blinding twigs. Even better than goggles are the transparent shields available as options on some helmets. A face mask is a big help, and I have found the felt masks worn by the Navy on North Atlantic duty far superior than wool masks. Helmets are vital to safety, and also the warmest headgear you will find.

Snowmobile clothing cannot be topped, both the one-piece and the two-piece outfits. If your choice is a two-piece, make certain the trousers fit high and are bibbed.

Sleeves should be finished with a knitted cuff or a storm cuff—preferably a storm cuff because it will not be subjected to much wear or stretch when inside a nylon sleeve.

Play it cool when your snowmobile becomes bogged in a drift, mired in slush or trapped in a hole. You cannot wrestle one of these brutes without inviting injury. Backs are especially vulnerable—I know.

When my machine became stuck in deep snow while on a trip in the far north, I tried to manhandle it out of its predicament without using my legs—or head. I was almost lifted out of my suit by the pain of a hundred toothaches. It was as if someone had jabbed a six-inch spike in my spine.

Fortunately, my companion was nearby and having helped me to a nearby road, he returned and rescued my snowmobile. I had an angular look for a few days, and my carelessness put a damper on our outing.

When badly stuck, dig free with a snowshoe and stamp a path back to a solid base. When you lift it, take it easy and let your legs do the work.

A small block and tackle is a clever item to pack, and might someday spell the difference between "freezing in the clutches" and hoofing it; or driving back. With the snowmobile's speed and mobility, you can find yourself in trouble many miles from home base.

As with all mechanical contraptions, a snowmobile is capable of wheezing its last anywhere, anytime. The problem may be too complex for even the most skilled snowbank mechanic, or he may lack the necessary tools or parts.

When yesteryear's winter traveler became injured, ill or blizzard-bound, he tossed a sled-dog into the cooking pot and pulled the rest of the team on top of him for warmth. However, those days are gone.

As one Indian put it: "Snowmobile okay, but ever try to eat a carburetor?"

I was given a cheap lesson on the need for a survival kit, which convinced me not to venture forth again without one.

We were lost in a blinding blizzard which had obliterated the tracks our snowmobiles had made hours earlier when we had struck off into the wilderness. The mercury was plummeting and darkness was descending.

We cruised the perimeter of the forest, hoping desperately to spot a recognizable landmark. As we were about to make the best of our plight and dig in for the night, we spotted a flicker of light through the swirling white curtain.

It was winking through the tiny window of a twelve-foot square cubicle occupied by a couple of trappers and their wives—truly emancipated females who snowshoed the lines setting traps and snares; then skinned the carcasses of the creatures they caught. It is said that horses sweat, men perspire and women glow —these two certainly had an unmistakable after-glow. But they were a happy quartet, and some 30 minutes after they pointed us in the right direction we happily arrived at base camp, none the worse for our experience.

When I returned to civilization, I tried to purchase

a suitable survival kit, but was unable to find one. The kits on the shelves came from Tokyo or Madison Avenue and were inadequate and/or bulky.

So, I built my own tested lifesaver, which is compact, complete and relatively inexpensive. "Tested?" That's right. I put it through its paces one frosty night — and lived to tell the tale. While it was a simulated emergency lacking the psychological stresses present in a genuine crisis, the kit came through with flying colors.

The container is a mess kit comprised of a pot, a dish and a frying pan, measuring only 6-inches x 6-inches x 3-inches. But it is large enough to accommodate the following thirty items.

First aid supplies include a "how to" booklet, codeine pills, antiseptic, salve, band-aids, forty-inch bandage, wire splint and adhesive tape. The larder consists of chocolate, fruit/nut bars, beef bouillon cubes, packaged soup and glucose tablets.

Waxed matches are backed up by a "metal match", which will ignite several thousand times. It is sparked when struck by the kit's pocket knife.

Firewood and the framework for a lean-to are easily cut with the survival kit's wire bandsaw, which resembles a short length of barbed wire with a ring on both ends.

A 54-inch x 84-inch "rescue blanket" roofs the shelter. The layered metallic foil reflects the fire's heat, and is easily spotted from above. A second "rescue blanket" serves as a sleeping bag.

Other aids are a metal signalling mirror, and a pencil-size flare gun with nine rounds.

The enclosed thumb tacks are used to attach the roof of the lean-to to its frame. Also included are

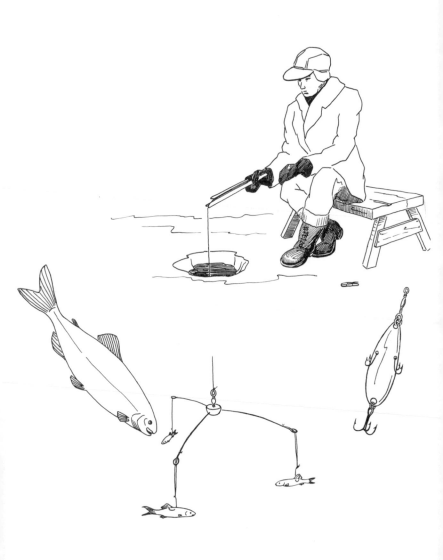

multi-use safety pins, thirty feet of nylon rope, four candles and a compass. This kit is a potential lifeline which warrants a place in every outdoorsman's outfit.

The ecological impact of the snowmobile has been exaggerated by its oponents. The majority of mature users drive sanely, but there are yahoos in this activity, as in any other one. The bad apples harass wildlife, crush young trees, and annoy local residents.

While noise has been a headache since the inception of snowmobiles, the manufacturers say, "it's too bad, but there is nothing we can do." Hogwash—decibels are now being lowered through legislation, which unfortunately appears to be the only effective silencer. The manufacturers have demonstrated an irresponsible attitude during the entire growth of the industry. Take horsepower for example.

It has been promoted as a great feature. Do not believe it. You will be safer and have just as much fun on a snowmobile shy on horses by today's varrooom yardstick.

This vehicle has provided the snow camper with first-class transportation to his site, just as the car or boat does at other times of year; and it affords an opportunity for some diversion while in camp.

Since most provinces and states have regulations governing the operation and registration of snowmobiles, don't tow across the borders without familiarizing yourself with the laws of the area you are visiting.

WINTER DIET

Planning the snow-camping larder is easy, but not as simple to do as is the fair-weather larder. I have no intention of spelling out a menu which, of course, would require adjustment according to the number of mouths, individual tastes and/or allergies, and length of stay.

I am a far cry from a creator of culinary masterpieces, which my wife and other camping companions will readily endorse. They call me a "survival cook", which means that you dig into my mealtime disasters only when the alternative is starvation.

Keep the furnace stoked and your house will be warm. Not profound, but true. Just remember that your body is your house and your stomach is the furnace.

Eat a lot and eat often, is a good guideline for comfortable snow camping. Frigid weather and the exertion of moving through the white stuff will sap your energy and encourage the chills.

Always stuff a few chocolate bars, cheese and raisins in your pockets to nibble on when you feel hungry, weary or chilled.

Include plenty of protein in your camp diet. One reason that the Eskimo can withstand the extreme Arctic winters is because of the large quantity of meat which he consumes.

Beef stew, chili con carne, corned beef hash, chicken with rice are but a few meals which can be prepared in advance at home, packed in plastic containers and frozen. Pop them into the cooking pot and you will be eating within minutes.

Some of the freeze-dried "meals in a packet" are delicious, nutritious, and very worthwhile when back-packing.

Catch a fish from the icy waters of a frozen lake and you will be in for a genuine taste treat. Flavor is tops and flesh is firm. If ice fishing is on the camping itinerary, be optimistic enough to tote all the makings of a

glimpse at the long and the short of the
often encountered by campers.

more likely to get into difficulties with the
pasture than with the bull of the woods.
rtainly attain awesome proportions. Those
nd the Yukon may weigh three quarters of
an antler spread of five to six feet.
be a formidable animal with which to
to face if it happened to be an aggressive
er. Happily, that is not the case.
ose chase you? The answer is an emphatic
the possible exception of a mother moose
s her calf is in danger. The protective in-
otherhood is a very powerful force in most
from the smallest to the largest.
on those autumnal moose hunts when we
d on "track soup" instead of steaks, I have
hed that moose would occasionally pursue
d of me forever trying to catch up to them.
noe-camper is more likely to see them than is
unter. The camper is usually on the scene at
of year when black flies are putting the run
easts. Once in the cool waters of a northern
iver they are loath to get out of the swim and
clouds of flies on shore.
evening moose are frequently spotted along
eline, feeding on the tender young roots of the
ly.
ng a May excursion into a tiny lake we viewed
tanding belly-deep, all at the same time.
t a photographic opportunity! Moose have
usly poor eyesight and are no great shakes at
ying a motionless object, although movement

fish fry except the vital one. These are salt, pepper, lemon juice, flour and cooking oil or butter.

Do not take canned foods, fresh fruit and vegetables, eggs and tinned or bottled beverages. With the exception of the basic ingredient of a before-bed hot toddy, they will all freeze.

To capsule "snowtime chowtime" make it hot, meaty, generous and frequent.

W

MOOSE

You are
bull of the
Moose ce
in Alaska a
a ton with
It would
come face
people-ha
Will mo
NO, with
who think
stinct of
creatures,
In fact
have dine
often wis
me instea
The ca
the fall h
the time
on the b
lake or
face the
In th
the sho
water l
Duri
seven
Wha
notori
identif

No, not the neighbors in
loudly after decent folks
the next campsite who
day.

I refer to residents of th
er, howl, rustle and go bu

Wildlife is misunderst
self-ordained experts. On
tures with fear or abhorren
them lovable inhabitants o
characteristics.

Both are far off base. Mu
from observing the fascinatin
world. While they are not t
harbor a healthy respect for
inflicting injury. Watch them
graph them, but don't try to
wild animals any favors by di
fear of humans.

If you must feed the anima
outs to the chipmunks and bi

113

will quickly spook them. By paddling frantically when a bull had its head below decks in the feed bucket, and freezing when he raised his velvet-covered vegetation-draped antlers, we were able to come within a paddle stroke of the Gargantuan, shooting pictures all the while. At that point my bowman, being some 15 feet nearer than I, decided that that was close enough. When he backpaddled, a very startled moose galloped toward the tall timber.

You will sometimes discover a moose trail girdling a wilderness lake. It may angle into the woods to re-appear farther down the shore at another "snack bar".

By stationing yourself beside this path, you may snap some outstanding photos of moose on the hoof. Believe me, it is nerve-wracking to come face to face with one, no matter how many you have seen at a distance.

Except during the autumn rut, the monarch of the forest is a timid type.

DEER

Deer are nocturnal creatures, and are most fre-quently spotted by campers logging some after-dark hours behind the wheel. Their eyes will sparkle like re-flectors in the glare of the car's headlights. Take it easy, as they may bound in front of your vehicle at the last minute or, blinded by your lights, stand bewil-dered in the middle of the road. A wrecked car is some-thing you can do without at any time, but especially while on vacation.

Deer in some state and provincial parks become spoiled by tourists' handouts, and learn to stand by the road like beggars.

"Bambi" has spawned a lot of cockeyed notions

about these animals. Don't let those big brown eyes fool you. They are not always gentle, docile and harmless. Their antlers could skewer you, and their sharp hoofs could rip you open or pound you to pulp.

It has happened.

Surprise deer drinking at the water's edge and they will be gone in a flash, white flags waving goodbye.

In many of the large parks where deer once abounded, they have become scarce. Why? It cannot be because of an over-harvest by hunters, since no hunting is the general rule in government parks.

A diminished habitat is probably the answer. Logging operations may have ceased, or may have been scaled down because of the public's desire to see parklands returned to a natural state.

Returning parkland to a natural state is a meritorious objective, for there is very little unspoiled wilderness close to the beaten track. But remember, we cannot have mature forests and abundant wildlife too. They don't go hand-in-hand. Once the forest canopy shuts out the sunlight, lush young ground growth disappears and with it much of the wildlife. Their cupboard is bare.

While harassing deer is deemed cruel, giving them handouts is just as heartless. If this is what nature intended, the woods would be filled with popcorn bushes and candy bar trees.

THE WILD CANINES

Chances are you will go through life without setting eyes on a wolf or a coyote, except for that miserable creature pacing its cell in the local zoo.

But if you camp a lot, sooner or later you will hear them and it is a spine-tingling thrill. The baying of a wolf pack will raise the hair on your neck and the goose bumps on your flesh. They howl at the moon for the sake of doing it, or to communicate with one another across miles of hushed and darkened woodlands.

My most memorable experience was when I heard a howling pack hot on the heels of a potential meal— probably a deer. The yelping and yipping grew louder and nearer and more frenzied until shivers shot through me as I sat bolt upright in my sleeping bag. When they were within a quarter of a mile of me, a sudden silence signalled that they had killed their quarry.

The next morning a reconnoitre in the woods uncovered the scattered remains of a doe, most of which had been devoured.

While the timber wolf is extinct over most of its former United States range, there is no scarcity of coyotes—often called "brush wolves". The wolf is not as dangerous as Rover, who sometimes bites the postman. If a wolf spots the postman or any other human, it goes like a streak.

The only persons they devour are the children pitched off sleighs, as depicted by the artists of yesteryear.

In Ontario's Algonquin Park, wolf-howling safaris are led by park naturalists armed with recordings and amplifiers. As many as 1200 campers have gathered in the dark to listen to the howls of live wolves replying to the records.

Those yipyip yips you will hear in the black beyond are not wolf sounds. They are made by a fox barking at the moon. This is especially prevalent during the early spring mating season.

The wolf is neither black nor white in color or

character. Old lobo is a grey animal. But we should hope that he will keep his toehold in the shrinking wilderness where he will continue to thrill campers with his eerie, tremulous "call of the wild".

BEARS

"Jasper" and "Smokey" have created a false image of a mischievous, fun-loving, human-like fellow in a furry black parka. Bears may be affable at times, but they are also totally unpredictable.

There are countless stories of campers being seriously injured by bears. Their shearing claws, see-saw dispositions, murderous jaws and incredible strength can spell big trouble. Campers will remember for a long time the tragic deaths of the youngsters who were literally devoured by grizzlies in a western park.

Yet the stupidity perpetuates. A flabbergasted park ranger spotted a tourist trying to shove a 300-pound bear into his automobile so that he could snap a funny picture to show to the folks back home.

And another tourist was nearly decapitated when he got down on all fours to mimic a bear, which reciprocated by swatting him with one of its lethal paws.

One fellow fed a bear candies which he extracted from his hip pocket one at a time. When the supply was exhausted the bear's appetite was not. The bear decided to look for more goodies where the others had come from, which resulted in a lengthy tenure in a hospital for the candy man. I suppose that could be called "biting the ass that feeds you".

As the signs say, "Don't Feed the Bears!" If they are standing beside the road and you want to stop for a look, keep the car windows rolled up. If you are driving a convertible, keep going.

People who feed bears around campgrounds are asking for trouble, for themselves and the bruins. Bears will soon lose all fear of man, and will wreak havoc around a camping area.

They will rip tents apart, smash food boxes, and dump every garbage can in the place.

If they have become a nuisance where you camp, keep your grub in the trunk of the car, wipe away all traces of food from the picnic table and, if necessary, hang food from a rope over the limb of a nearby tree.

Although their eyesight is poor, their sense of smell is excellent.

The time-worn advice about not getting between a sow bear and her cubs is very valid. Steer clear of those cuddly babies.

Should a bear invade your camp, bang on some pots and pans, yell your head off, but do not try to shoo it away with a stick or broom. It might be your final act of aggression.

RACCOONS

Wearing their black masks, these animals look like the camp robbers they are. Mind you, the potlickers will save the washing-up brigade from dishwater hands. Just leave the unwashed supper pans and dishes sitting outside, and you will see what I mean.

You will be awakened in the night by a clatter and rattle, and there, caught red-handed in the beam of your flashlight, will be a raccoon dining off your leftovers.

While that is not serious, a racoon who invades camp in your absence can leave a maddening mess in his wake. The clever thief will pry the lids off tins, solve the food box combination and gnaw through plastic, cardboard and paper to get at the contents of a package.

Raccoons will hang on for a final mouthful, even at the sound of your approach, and you may spot a ringed tail scooting around a corner of the tent when you are within steps of it.

But that is not all. They will steal your plastic-bagged catch of trout from the bottom of the spring hole, even if you have weighted it down with a big boulder. And all fish left overnight on the stringer will be goners too. If the raccoons don't find them, the turtles will.

Raccoons are nocturnal creatures and do most of their prowling after dark, spending the day curled up in a hollow stump, log or cave.

They are one of nature's most cooperative models, and if your camera is equipped with a flash unit, you can catch them in the act for posterity.

PORCUPINES

Nature's walking pincushion has been compensated for its sloth-like pace by being equipped with a formidable exterior. The porcupine is one of the more frequent campground visitors, usually an unwelcome one.

Its insatiable appetite for anything having the slightest trace of salt has spelled despair or disaster for many bushmen. They will chew paddles into pieces, devour axe handles, gnaw holes in canoes and boats and capsize buildings by eating the supports.

No Virginia, they don't toss their quills; but do be certain to steer a wide berth around their flailing tails. An imbedded quill is painful; its removal even more so. These spikes have ends like buttonhooks, which grip with tenacity once implanted.

While porcupines present no danger to campers, they are a real threat to vacationing household pets. The dog who has never encountered one will give chase just as it would with a cat. Fido's howls of anguish will tell you he has caught one. His tender nose and his mouth will probably be bristling with quills.

If possible, take the dog to a veterinarian, who will extract the quills while the mutt is anesthetized. If this cannot be done, you will have to tackle the job yourself with a pair of strong pliers.

A word of caution. Dogs are not appreciative of the good deed you are performing, so make certain the dog is belted or tied securely. Enlist the aid of others to help pin the patient during the operation.

Bright lights and loud noises will frighten porcupines off. Frequently they will waddle only as far as the first tree, which they will scale with no difficulty.

If these creatures are common to the region where you are camping, take a few precautions; put the axe and paddles out of harm's way before turning in for the night.

SNAKES

Not a day passes without panic-stricken campers racing to the ranger with a story about the puff adder, water moccasion or copperhead snake which nearly nailed them. Sometimes they will show up with the pulverized carcass cautiously draped across the end of a long stick.

The innocent victims of their persecution are usually harmless hog-nosed, water, milk and even garter snakes.

North America has four poisonous species. The most venomous is the gold and black banded coral snake, which is confined to the swamplands of the deep south.

The cottonmouth or water moccasin occupies the same territory as the coral snake, although it does range a little further northward.

The greatest concentration of copperheads is in the dry rocky country of the southwest, although they are found in fewer numbers in some parts of the southeast.

The other pit viper is the rattlesnake, of which the most dangerous is the diamond back, and the least harmful the massasauga.

None spell instant death, and the treatment for bites is described in the First Aid section of this book.

Snakes don't look for trouble, and if you exercise a watchful eye and sensible precautions when traveling their bailiwick you will be perfectly safe. It does make good sense to wear thick trousers tucked into high leather boots when hiking through country where rattlesnakes are common.

Our entire campsite was aroused early one night by the piercing shrieks of a female in distress. We converged on the source of the screams, where we met a very shaken young lady in her night attire, who stammered that she had discovered a snake in her sleeping bag.

To which an amused old-timer drawled "Don't be skeerd, ma'am. He only crawled in to get warm."

BABES IN THE WOODS

Most babes in the woods belong exactly where you have found them. They have not been abandoned on Mother Nature's doorstep.

While kids are understandably guilty of "adopting" any young wild creature they find, adults should know better.

The tiny dappled fawn curled in a clump of cover has not been forsaken by its mother. She will be back at mealtime for sure, and may be observing you at that very minute from among the protective foliage. Young deer, being virtually scentless and well camouflaged, are reasonably safe from most predators.

Moose moms and mother bears are not nearly so passive if they get the notion in their heads that you are going to harm their offspring.

Forget about trying to make a pet out of a wild animal. Few make a desirable addition to the family. Their inherent wildness is born into them and can seldom be removed by man's clumsy efforts to domesticate them.

There is nothing more pitiful and pathetic than the sight of a bear, deer, fox, or whatever, imprisoned for life in a tiny filthy cage as an attraction to "gas up". In a number of states and provinces this practice is now illegal. Let us hope others will follow suit.

Even if you have no intention of taking it home, by merely touching a young animal or bird, you may have killed it just as dead as if you had throttled it on the spot.

Whether from human scent, relocation or abnormal actions resulting from excitement or shock, baby birds and beasts will often be ignored by their parents, and thus they will be condemned to a slow, cruel death.

While the "Let It Be" slogan is usually brandished by the emotional and the uninformed, this is one instance where it does apply.

FIRST AID

Chapter Seven

FIRST AID

While camp injuries and ills are seldom serious by medical standards, if a camper is hours or days away from professional help, a minor ailment may become major before it is properly treated. While everyone should have a basic knowledge of first aid, it is imperative that the camper be thus informed. Your first-aid know-how could someday save a life; perhaps your own.

It's not that camp life is riddled with danger. You are a far sight safer on a boondock waterway than on a tarmac highway.

Rather than pass along this layman's treatments and remedies, I felt the subject warranted the advice of a physician. The medicine man I consulted is Dr. David Evans, an esteemed physician who graduated from England's University of Birmingham in 1956. He moved to Canada in 1960, where he is an assistant professor at the University of Toronto and on the staff at Western Hospital, in addition to conducting his own practice.

Best of all, the doctor is a keen, knowledgeable

outdoorsman; and a devotee of canoeing, camping and angling. Who better qualified to counsel kindred souls on treatments of aches, ailments, bites, breaks, burns and other injuries and maladies which sometimes kill camp-outs (and campers).

I found a peek into Dr. Evans' personal first-aid kit extremely interesting. I think you will too.

The doctor suggests substituting an ounce of prevention for the proverbial "apple a day".

He recommends skirting situations where unstable footing could result in bruises, sprains or broken bones.

This advice should be especially heeded by people who camp in mountainous regions. But there has been many a nasty header taken by waders in streams whose bottoms are littered with slimy boulders. The rocks along their edges are also treacherous after rains, or when high waters have receded. In cold weather, the seepage out of rocky slopes will freeze, leaving a nearly-invisible film of ice on its face. Beware of lichen which becomes slippery when wet, and moss on top of stone skids away underfoot in damp weather.

After dark, trails are hazardous pathways.

Dr. Evans stresses the need for caution with sharp objects such as knives, axes, saws and fish hooks. One of the worst offenders is the folding jack-knife. These should have a locking device so the blade cannot flip back down under pressure alone. Many fingers have been sliced to the bone by someone carelessly attempting to cut with the back of the blade, thus forcing the cutting edge onto the hand. Never leave belt knives lying around loose. Replace in their sheaths immediately.

While there are few serious accidents while saws are in use, they are frequently stuffed into a pack without a guard on the blade. Then someone reaches into the bag, emerging with a rough and bloody gash on hand or arm.

Axes can inflict a wound serious enough to be lethal, either from infection, shock or loss of blood. Always take the simple, but necessary, precautions when chopping or splitting. Keep your feet and legs well out of the path of your swing. Before you tackle your woodchopping chores, lop off any branches or surrounding brush which could deflect the axe.

I know whereof Dr. Evans speaks in respect to fishhooks. I have had many a barb in my hide, and have been forced to undergo bush surgery without the bottle of whisky inside, the six cowboys holding me down, and a stick clenched between my teeth, as depicted in wild west movies. In all but one case I was to blame, being too anxious to cast to a rise or too careless in handling a hooked fish.

The doctor suggests that if more people wore appropriate protective clothing when exposed to the elements, there would be fewer returning home ill or having to spend part of their vacation sick. Your wife is right when she emphatically "advises" you "don't go out in that weather without your hat on".

Drownings take a tragic toll of campers, usually because they were not garbed in a suitable life jacket. "Wear one at all times when you are on the water," says Dr. Evans, adding "even if you are a strong swimmer."

Overloading, unfamiliarity with tippy craft, and panic are three leading causes of drowning. The "stay with your boat" advice is good except when the water temperature approaches freezing point. Then exposure will quickly kill you unless you desert your swamped ship and strike for shore.

Food poisoning is serious, even when you are within minutes of medical attention and a stomach pump. But it can be murder in the wilderness. The doctor says "it is better to go hungry than to take chances with contaminated or stale food, particularly meat, milk and canned goods".

While Dr. Evans didn't exactly say cleanliness is next to godliness, he did emphasize that when you go camping do not leave the basic rules of hygiene at home.

There is nothing wrong with growing a beard in camp, if you still wash the face that's under it. If you don't have such amenities as hot showers and baths, settle for the cold versions under waterfalls or in lakes.

Always wash your hands before preparing food — and do the same with the pots it's cooked in and the plates it's eaten from.

His final words of caution "Have a high index of suspicion" sum up the situation. This boils down to "don't take unnecessary risks". Sound advice.

Here is a camper's mini medical journal, compiled with the cooperation and professional advice of Dr. Dave.

SCALDS AND BURNS

It happens all the time, either from sun, fire, boiling water, cooking pots or hot grease. The doctor is not an advocate of ointments. In fact he says "Don't apply any to the burned area, which will heal fastest when left exposed. Cold water on burned limbs will ease suffering. But in the case of serious burns, such as might occur if a tent caught on fire, a can of gasoline exploded, or if you were trapped by a forest fire, any clothing stuck to the burned skin and flesh should not be removed. In such cases, quick professional medical attention is imperative."

FRACTURES AND SPRAINS

They are a source of worry to hikers trekking rough terrain. In cases where balance could have been regained following a slip while walking without a burden, a heavy pack can make recovery impossible and down you go, possibly breaking an ankle or leg.

Sometimes a break and a bad sprain are indistinguishable externally. When in doubt, treat the injury as the more serious of the two. The first step is to apply splints, which the doctor points out not only sprout from every tree but also girdle them. A stiff piece of bark makes an excellent splint. Elastic bandages lend support to the injured limb, but take care not to apply them too tightly.

Finally, the injured person should rest, and avoid putting stress on the injury and thus run the risk of compounding the problem.

BITES

The likelihood of a camper being bitten by an animal is slim. However, it can happen if the creature is rabid, cornered, or if young animals are handled. A baby raccoon will often respond to misguided human affection with a nasty nip.

An animal bite should be thoroughly disinfected and dealt with like any other laceration, unless there is a possibility that the biter was rabid. Rabies can kill if you don't receive the necessary innoculations to counteract its effects.

Even non-poisonous snakes will sometimes bite,

but this is not serious if the shallow wound or scratch is cleansed. If bitten by one of the venomous species, the bite should be sliced open, the poison removed by suction and a tourniquet applied between bite and heart. Snake bite kits contain the necessary items. Lacking one of these, the wound should be sucked clean by mouth. Hot drinks help, but the legendary "snake bite kits", which are packed in quart bottles, do a lot of harm. Don't drink alcohol for it speeds the circulation. Avoid strenuous activity, stay calm and quiet, and head for civilization. Most hospitals in snake country carry a supply of antivenom serum.

The doctor prescribes antihistamines for insect bites, and suggests that those who are allergic to bee stings (and those who don't know if they are) should carry a bee sting kit which consists of adrenalin, syringes and an instruction booklet.

DIARRHOEA

While his preferred remedy is Kaomylin, Dr. Evans advises a search for the cause. Check the larder for spoiled food, and if there is a chance that your drinking water may be contaminated, boil it, or treat it with purifying tablets such as halazone.

To go to the other extreme, the doctor warns against the use of laxatives unless you are certain that constipation is the cause of your discomfort. Apparently, an inflamed appendix is only one of the internal problems which can produce symptoms similar to those of acute constipation. As with most things, laxatives should be taken in moderation.

SUNSTROKE

The external symptoms are those of a severe sunburn, accompanied by nausea and possibly dizziness. The urbanite is inclined to grab his sunshine in big doses when the rare opportunity presents itself. This is a mistake.

Don't leave your head exposed to the hot sun for long periods. Wear a hat, but not one of those mesh types which shade the eyes while allowing the sun to beat mercilessly on your dome.

In the event of sunstroke, the best cure is rest in the cool shade.

TOOTHACHE

An aching tooth can be a real vacation spoiler, and cannot be cured short of the dentist's drill or forceps. Toothaches frequently turn a pleasant outing into a painful ordeal. Why? It might be because circulation is increased by chopping, portaging or backpacking. Dr. Evans says to ease the pain with codeine pills and to apply warmth and oil of cloves to the offending tooth.

BLEEDING

Pressure is the tactic to employ to stop bleeding, and a tourniquet should be used only as a last resort if the flow of blood cannot be checked by other means.

My professional consultant mentioned that amputations have been necessary in many cases where a tourniquet was left tightened too long. It must be released within thirty minutes to preclude the possibility of killing a limb.

Many people get nosebleeds without warning in or out of camp. A cold compress over the nose will cause constriction of the blood vessels and should stop the flow.

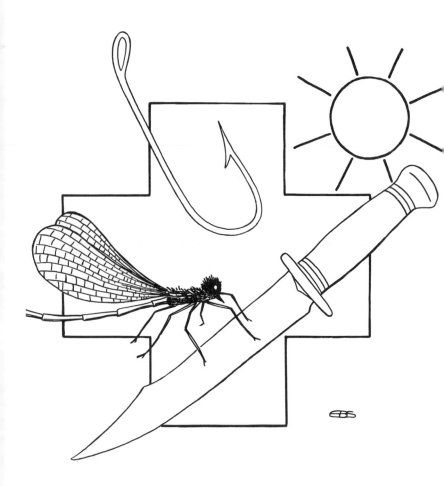

IRRITATED EYES

It is not unusual to get a foreign body in your eye around the campsite. Grit, sawdust or insects are the common culprits.

A simple operation is to place a matchstick on the upper eyelid, then roll it upwards like a window blind and try to spot the source of irritation. If you see the problem, try to remove it with a piece of cotton wool or tissue.

Here's a sleeper. Before attempting the surgery outlined above, pull the upper eyelid over the lower and blow your nose. According to the good doctor it often solves the problem.

BRUISES

Most of us have been bruised and battered throughout life, but those internal injuries cannot be rectified even by surgery. Just as time heals life's bruises, it will do the same for the black and blue variety which appear under your skin if you have been thumped physically. A cold compress will hasten their demise, as will a coating of vaseline. The vaseline cure mystifies the doctor, but he vouches for its effectiveness.

LACERATIONS

We have all sustained such injuries at some time or other. The edge of a tin can, a piece of broken glass, or the blade of a knife will all slice swiftly. The cut should be cleansed with iodine, then taped together. In the case of large lacerations, Dr. Evans says "Clench your teeth and suture the wound". Ouch!

HOOKS

When you get one of these in your hide, you wonder

how a fish is ever able to shake them. Those barbs really grip! Forget about backing them out again. The route to follow is "onward and upward", like the Boy's Brigade. From experience, I suggest that you don't dally, but get on with the job. When the barb reappears, snip it off with wire cutting pliers and back the remains out the way it entered.

Do not attempt surgery if a hook is lodged in a critical part of the anatomy. Cut it off as close to the skin as possible and make tracks for the surgeon's scalpel and a local anaesthetic. An anti-tetanus shot is also in order.

SHOCK

Shock is an aftermath of one of the foregoing problems, and is easily diagnosed. Cold, clammy skin, a rapid pulse and a feeling of apprehension are all indicative. Shock can prove to be more serious than the injury.

Persons suffering from shock will feel cold, and should be made comfortable and warm; but not hot. The doctor says moral support will do more good than medication.

COLDS AND FLU

Do the same things as you would at home, minus the hot bath, of course. While colds and flu usually take their course, rest, fluids and aspirins will help speed them on their way.

PAIN

Pain resulting from fractures, bites, blood loss, etc., can be partially subdued by codeine tablets. In extreme cases, Dr. Evans prescribes a vial of morphine

(15 mg.) injected into the shoulder muscle.

Anyone contemplating a fly-in, hike-in, or paddle-in, who suffers from a heart condition, stomach ulcers, diabetes or other ailments requiring a complicated drug routine, should check with his physician before making final arrangements.

People allergic to drugs—such as penicillin—should wear a bracelet containing that information. These bracelets are available from the Medic Alert Foundation.

In the case of cessation of breathing and/or heartbeat due to drowning, lightning or smoke inhalation, artificial respiration should commence immediately.

Here's a step-by-step procedure, as explained by Dr. Evans:

1. Clear the mouth of any foreign matter, including dentures.
2. Place the victim on his back and tilt head backwards.
3. Place your mouth over the victim's, raise chin and pinch nose.
4. Blow every four to five seconds, and watch the chest rise and fall.
5. If there is no response within a minute, thump the lower half of the breast bone sharply several times with the butt of your hand.
6. Resume artificial respiration by inflating the chest with two mouth-to-mouth breaths.
7. If there is still no response, begin external cardiac massage.
8. With the victim stretched on a firm surface, place the heel of one hand on the bottom third of the breast bone and press your other hand over the first.

9. With arms straight, press firmly fifteen times at a rate of seventy times per minute.
10. Alternate fifteen chest compressions with two mouth-to-mouth breaths. Continue until the victim revives, or death is a certainty.

THE KIT

Most ingredients in the doctor's personal first-aid kit won't be found in the $2.98 drug store specials. He suggests you follow his example, and assemble your own. However, some components can be obtained only on prescription from your family physician.

Bandages

(a) four gauze roller bandages in three or four inch widths
(b) twelve two-inch-square gauze pads
(c) one package of band-aids
(d) one triangular bandage
(e) two three-inch elastic bandages

Instruments

(a) one pair of surgical forceps
(b) one pair of tweezers
(c) one pair of small scissors
(d) two surgical sutures and pre-packed needles
(e) two 3 c.c. hypodermic syringes and pre-packed needles

Drugs

(a) 100 aspirin
(b) twelve ounces Kaolin or Kaomylin
(c) one ounce 2% iodine
(d) one tube antibiotic eye ointment (sulpha)

(e) one tube anaesthetic eye ointment

(f) eighteen 4 mg. Chlor-Tripolon (anti-histamine) pills

(g) six 100 mg. codeine tablets

(h) twelve vials 15 mg. morphine

(i) one tube anaesthetic jelly

Snake Bite Kit

Bee Sting Kit

Thermometer

Brooks Airway (a two-way airway for mouth-to-mouth resuscitation).

Chapter Eight

LEAVE ONLY YOUR FOOTPRINTS

A recent magazine article advised the camper/photographer, "add dimension to your pictures by framing them with natural surroundings". But the author's idea of "natural surroundings" included vehicles, picnic tables, and people!

A generous reaction would be to credit the writer with farsightedness, and looking ahead to the turn of the century.

How "modern man" has botched the whole show! He has contaminated the air and polluted the waters. He has ruthlessly felled forests to the last tree, which he labels "clear cutting". And then he has the audacity to term it "sound conservation". He has exterminated many species of wildlife and sickened others.

Mankind gobbles the non-renewable natural resources as though there were no tomorrow. At the present rate of pollution, that might not be far from the truth.

The Good Earth is being milked of her all. Gas, oil, minerals and coal are being skinned off her hide and siphoned from her bowels.

Wildlife is retreating ahead of the bulldozer and power saws. Fish are turning belly-up in cesspools once called lakes. One-time waterfowl breeding grounds, now wave with wheat, are dotted with cattle, or are paved with asphalt.

And the dam builders continue to further their insatiable desires to throttle the life from the rivers. And this carnage goes under the guise of "progress".

Definitions of progress can be poles apart. The yardstick many people today use is made from concrete, smokestacks and asphalt.

A truer meaning of "progress" is mankind's attitude, ability to think clearly, and accurately foresee tomorrow's potential problems. Most of us will have gone to that bivouac in the sky when our environmental bumbling, meddling and destruction will have its catastrophic impact.

And if man is still on this planet in a hundred, or even fifty years, will he look back and applaud our progressive thinking? Not very likely.

We haven't the right to punder a heritage which also belongs to those as yet unborn. Non-renewable resources should be used sparingly by all who pass this way, but no one has the right to exhaust them.

Recently, a monstrous scheme which would jam thousands of skiers into a pocket of precious parkland, complete with discotheques, etc., had tentative governmental blessing. When a groundswell of angry public opposition scuttled the ship, one of those aboard angrily asked: "Are parks for people or for birds?" Cities are for people, parks are for birds and people.

Parks should not be museums, but should be used and enjoyed unchanged by hikers, campers, naturalists, fishermen and hunters.

Our countryside is pocked with such blights as the panorama of billboards, automobile graveyards heaped high with rusty corpses, and sprawling smog-shrouded urbanism shorn of every tree.

We must save what's left, and defend it with stoic determination from further desecration. Let rivers run wild, free and unpolluted. Let skies be blue again and allow at least a part of our forests to grow tall, safe from the woodsman's axe.

Ignore ivory-towered self-ordained experts who see the wilderness as a wasteland to exploit, or as a Disneyland to be fenced in. Big Brother is far from infallible.

The ponderous pace of government must accelerate to stabilize teetering environments before they collapse.

Misuse and abuse of our wilderness and parklands often spring from a humble beginning. One careless camper infects others. Pitch your garbage and so will the next guy. Take it back and he will too.

Out with hotdog stands, off with blaring transistor radios, zilch to portable T.V. tubes. Nowadays you can take it with you, but why would anyone want to?

Don't spew a trail of civilization's excrement to prick the bubble of happiness of those who will follow you. Every litter bit hurts. Leave each campsite cleaner than you found it.

If our grandchildren are to experience the wonders of the great outdoors, canoe a wild river, hike a remote trail, catch trout, flush grouse or sit by a campfire, the turning point must be now.

Will the sight of a soaring eagle and the sound of a laughing loon be but echoes in old ears and nostalgia in old minds?

The great outdoors must be guarded from the ravages

Chapter Nine

WHERE TO GO

WHERE TO WRITE FOR MAPS AND INFORMATION

ALABAMA
Department of Conservation and Natural Resources
64 N. Union Street, Montgomery 36104

ALASKA
Department of Natural Resources
Pouch M. Goldstein Bldg., Juneau 99801

ARIZONA
Land Department
400 State Office Bldg., Phoenix 85007

ARKANSAS
Department of Parks and Tourism
149 State Capital, Little Rock 72201

CALIFORNIA
The Resources Agency
Department of Parks and Recreation
1416 Ninth Street, Sacramento 95814

COLORADO
Department of Natural Resources
1845 Sherman, Denver 80203

CONNECTICUT
State Park and Forest Commission
Rm. 273, State Office Bldg., Hartford 96115

DELAWARE
Department of Natural Resources and Environmental Control
Div. of Parks, Recreation and Forestry
The Edward Tathall Bldg., Legislative Ave. and D Street
Dover 19901

FLORIDA
Department of Natural Resources
Division of Parks and Recreation
Larson Building, Gaines St. at Monroe
Tallahassee 32301

GEORGIA
Department of State Parks
7th Fl., 270 Washington St. S.W., Atlanta 30334

IDAHO
Department of Parks
Statehouse, Boise 83707

ILLINOIS
Department of Conservation
102 State Office Bldg., Springfield 62706

INDIANA
Department of Natural Resources
608 State Office Bldg., Indianapolis 46204

IOWA
State Conservation Commission
State Office Bldg., 300 4th St., Des Moines 50319

KANSAS
Joint Council on Recreation

Park and Resources Authority, 801 Harrison, Topeka 66612

KENTUCKY
Department of Parks
State Office Building Annex, Frankfort 40601

LOUISIANA
State Parks and Recreational Commission
P.O. Drawer 1111, Baton Rouge 70821

MAINE
Department of Natural Resources
State Office Bldg., Augusta 04330

MARYLAND
Department of Forests and Parks
State Office Bldg., Annapolis 21401

MASSACHUSETTS
Department of Natural Resources
Division of Forests and Parks
Leverett Saltonstall Bldg., 100 Cambridge Street., Boston 02202

MICHIGAN
Department of Natural Resources
Mason Bldg., Lansing 48926

MINNESOTA
Department of Natural Resources
Division of Parks and Recreation
301 Centennial Bldg., 658 Cedar St., St. Paul 55101

MISSISSIPPI
Park System
717 Robert E. Lee Bldg., Jackson 39201

MISSOURI
State Park Board
Rm. 1204, Jefferson Bldg., Box 176, Jefferson City 65101

MONTANA
Department of State Lands
Capitol Building, Helena 59601

NEBRASKA
Game and Parks Commission
Bureau of State Parks
2200 N. 33rd St., P.O. Box 30370, Lincoln 68509

NEVADA
Department of Conservation and Natural Resources
Division of State Parks
Nye Bldg., Carson City 89701

NEW HAMPSHIRE
Department of Resources and Economic Development
Division of Parks
State House Annex, Concord 03301

NEW JERSEY
Department of Environmental Protection
Division of Parks and Forests
Labor and Industry Bldg., Box 1390, Trenton 08625

NEW MEXICO
State Park and Recreation Commission
P.O. Box 1147, Santa Fe 87501

NEW YORK
Department of Environmental Conservation
50 Wolf Road, Albany 12201
and
New York State Executive Department
Office of Parks and Recreation
The South Mall, Albany 12223

NORTH CAROLINA
Department of Conservation and Development
P.O. Box 27687, Raleigh 27611

NORTH DAKOTA
State Park Service
Rt. 2, Box 139, Mandan 58554

OHIO
Department of Natural Resources
Div. of Parks and Recreation
907 Ohio Departments Bldg., Columbus 43215

OKLAHOMA
Industrial Development and Park Department
Div. of Parks, Recreation and Waterways
500 Will Rogers Memorial Bldg., Oklahoma City 73105

OREGON
State Highways Division
State Parks and Recreation Section
State Highway Bldg., Salem 97310

PENNSYLVANIA
Department of Environmental Resources
Bureau of State Parks
Public Relations, Rm. 522, South Office Bldg., Harrisburg 17120

RHODE ISLAND
Department of Natural Resources
Division of Parks and Recreation
83 Park St., Providence 02903

SOUTH CAROLINA
Department of Parks, Recreation and Tourism
Division of State Parks
Box 1358, Columbia 29202

SOUTH DAKOTA
Department of Game, Fish and Parks
State Office Bldg., Pierre 57501

TENNESSEE
Department of Conservation
Division of State Parks
2611 W. End Ave., Nashville 37203

TEXAS
Parks and Wildlife Department
John H. Reagan Bldg., Austin 78701

UTAH
State Department of Natural Resources
Division of Parks and Recreation
1596 West North Temple, Salt Lake City

VERMONT
Agency of Environmental Conservation
Department of Forests and Parks
Montpelier 05602

VIRGINIA
Department of Conservation and Economic Development
Division of Parks
1201 State Office Bldg., Richmond 23219

WASHINGTON
State Parks and Recreation Commission
7150 Cleanwater La., P.O. Box 1128, Olympia 98504

WEST VIRGINIA
Department of Natural Resources
1800 Washington Street, East, Charleston 25305

WISCONSIN
Department of Natural Resources
Bureau of Parks and Recreation
Box 450, Madison 53701

WYOMING
Recreation Commission
P.O. Box 309, Cheyenne 82001

CANADA

ALBERTA
Department of Lands and Forests
Natural Resources Bldg., Edmonton 6

BRITISH COLUMBIA
Department of Recreation and Conservation
Parliament Bldgs., Victoria

MANITOBA
Department of Tourism, Recreation and Cultural
Affairs
Tourist Branch Room 408, Norquay Bldg.
Winnipeg 1

NEW BRUNSWICK
Department of Natural Resources
Tourism Development Branch, P.O. Box 1030,
Fredericton

NEWFOUNDLAND
Director of Parks
Resources Branch, Department of Mines, Agriculture
and Resources
St. John's

NORTHWEST TERRITORIES
Department of Industry and Development
Yellowknife

NOVA SCOTIA
Department of Lands and Forests
P.O. Box 68, Truro

ONTARIO
Ministry of Natural Resources
Parks and Recreation Branch
Queens Park, Toronto
PRINCE EDWARD ISLAND
Department of Environment and Tourism
P.O. Box 2000, Charlottetown
QUEBEC
Ministry of Tourism, Fish and Game
Parks Branch, Hotel du Gouvernement, Quebec City
SASKATCHEWAN
Department of Natural Resources
Park Development, Government Administration
Bldg., Regina
YUKON
Department of Travel and Information
Box 2703, Whitehorse

ACKNOWLEDGEMENTS

The author gratefully acknowledges the assistance given him by a large number of state and provincial officials who promptly returned completed questionnaires and contributed up-to-date camping data on regions under their jurisdiction. They are: In the United States: Mr. Reynolds W. Thrasher, Alabama; Mr. Theodore G. Smith, Alaska; Mr. Dennis McCarthy and Mr. Michael J. Pastika, Arizona; Mr. Max Love, Arkansas; Mr. George T. O'Malley, Colorado; Mr. William F. Miller, Connecticut; Mr. Wm. Hopkins and Mr. Earl Fenton, Delaware; Mr. Ney C. Landrum, Florida; Mr. George T. Bagby and Mr. Lowen Schuett, Idaho; Mr. R. P. Peterson, Idaho; Mr. Ronald D. Johnson and Ms. Betty P.

Guyer, Illinois; Mr. David L. Herbst and Mr. David S. Griffith, Indiana; Mr. Joe Brill, Iowa; Mr. Lynn Burris, Jr., Kansas; Mr. S. W. Palmer-Ball, Kentucky; Mr. Lamar Gibson, Louisiana; Mr. William H. Johnson, Maryland; Mr. Bruce S. Gullion, Massachusetts; Mr. O. J. Scherschligt and Mr. Kerr Stewart, Michigan; Mr. U. W. Hella, Minnesota; Mr. Spencer E. Medlin, Mississippi; Mr. Joseph Jaeger, Jr., Missouri; Mr. Ted Schwinden, Montana; Mr. Eric R. Cronkhite, Nevada; Mr. George T. Hamilton, New Hampshire; Mr. James L. Dillard, New Mexico; Mr. Ed Moore and Mr. F. W. Fuller, New York; Mr. Thomas C. Ellis and Mr. R. Gage Smith, North Carolina; Mr. David L. O'Brien, North Dakota; Mr. Norville Hall, Ohio; Mr. Tye Bledsoe and Mr. Robert A. Pike, Oklahoma; Mr. David G. Talbot, Oregon; Mr. Conrad R. Lickel, Pennsylvania; Mr. William H. Cotter, Jr., Rhode Island; Mr. Ray M. Sisk, South Carolina; Mr. James W. Sprague, South Dakota; Mr. W. T. Boswell, Tennessee; Mr. Richard A. McClune, Texas; Mr. Harold J. Tippetts and Mr. R. Clark Anderson, Utah; Mr. Rodney A. Barber, Vermont; Mr. Ben H. Bolen, Virginia; Mr. Charles H. Odegaard, Washington; Mr. Kermit McKeever, West Virginia; Mr. Milton E. Reinke and Mr. Rodney L. Nelson, Wisconson.

In Canada: Mr. Thomas A. Drinkwater and Mr. W. T. Galliver, Alberta; Mr. Robert Ahrens and Mr. Arthur E. Abram, British Columbia; Mr. W. E. Organ, Manitoba; Mr. D. K. Burtt, New Brunswick; Mr. Fred Gullage, Newfoundland; Mr. E. A. Ballantyne and Ms. E. Lennon, Northwest Territories; Mr. E. S. Atkins, Mr. W. R. Bryson, and Mr. H. J. A. Grant, Nova Scotia; Mr. J. Keenan, Ontario;

RESUMES OF STATE AND PROVINCIAL PARK FACILITIES

STATE/PROVINCE	NUMBER OF CAMPING PARKS	TOTAL ACREAGE	NUMBER OF CAMPSITES		RATES PER				CHARGED PER		WILDERNESS CAMPING PERMITTED
			SERVICED	UNSERVICED	DAY	WEEK	SEASON	PERSON	FAMILY	SITE	
U.S.A.											
Alabama*	5	—	—	—	2.00/3.00	—	—	—	—	✓	—
Alaska	47	498,818	837	837	2.00	—	—	—	✓	—	Yes
Arizona	5	23,240	163	196	1.75/2.25	—	—	—	—	✓	—
Arkansas	19	26,717	1,100	1,100	2.00/2.50	—	—	—	✓	✓	Yes
California	44	685,245	3,811	430	1.50/4.00	—	—	—	—	✓	No
Colorado	23	—	—	—	2.00+ park pass	—	—	—	—	✓ (car)	No
Connecticut	17	49,169	—	—	2.00/3.00	—	—	—	—	✓	No
Delaware	3	4,365	35	663	3.00/3.50	—	—	—	—	✓	No
Florida	36	37,810	2,500	—	4.00	—	—	—	—	✓	Yes
Georgia	35	—	1,575	420	2.50	—	—	—	✓	✓	Yes
Idaho	15	28,474	773	55	2.00/5.00	—	—	—	—	✓	Yes
Illinois	—	2,681,103	—	—	1.00/3.00	—	—	—	—	✓	Yes
Indiana	21	50,022	3,388	1,400	1.50/2.50	—	—	—	—	✓	No
Iowa	46	—	1,154	5,570	2.00/3.00	—	—	—	✓	—	—
Kansas	18	24,000	90	2,575	1.50	—	—	—	—	—	Yes
Kentucky	27	—	3,000	—	3.00	—	—	—	✓	—	Yes
Louisiana	9	12,256	694	319	1.30/2.80	—	—	—	✓	✓	—
Maine**	—	—	—	—	—	—	—	—	—	—	—
Maryland	18	25,000	1,573	—	3.50/4.00	24.50	—	—	—	—	Yes
Massachussetts	23	106,281	—	—	2.00/4.00	—	—	—	—	—	Yes
Michigan	70	202,000	12,704	2,110	1.50/3.00	—	—	—	—	✓	Yes
Minnesota	53	160,000	—	3,500	3.00	—	—	—	—	✓	No
Mississippi	15	15,439	450	—	2.50/3.00	—	—	—	—	✓	No
Missouri	30	70,000	653	2,865	2.00/3.00	—	—	—	—	✓	No
Montana	135	31,000	250	500	1.00	—	10.00	—	—	✓	Yes
Nebraska	14	—	—	—	1.50/2.00	—	—	—	—	✓	Yes
Nevada	12	110,000	302	6	2.00	—	15.00	—	✓	✓	Yes
New Hampshire	11	—	925	—	4.00	—	—	—	—	✓	—
New Jersey	7	17,993	124	240	—	—	—	—	—	—	No

158

New Mexico	26	85,000	260	520	2.00	—	—	20.00	✓	—	—	Yes
New York	60	177,900	2,925	5,831	2.50/3.00	—	—	—	✓	—	✓	No
North Carolina	9	58,000	—	—	2.00	10.00	—	—	—	—	✓	No
North Dakota	9	9,000	—	—	2.00	—	—	15.00	—	—	✓	Yes
Ohio	42	144,000	7,336	645	1.25/2.50	—	—	—	—	—	✓	No
Oklahoma	47	88,000	1,096	—	1.00/1.50	—	—	—	—	—	✓	No
Oregon	54	90,000	3,620	2,342	1.00/3.00	—	—	—	—	—	✓	Yes
Pennsylvania	45	3,108	5,298	5,298	2.00/3.00	—	—	—	—	—	✓	No
Rhode Island	5	5,416	105	903	2.00	14.00	—	—	—	—	✓	Yes
South Carolina	25	46,000	1,850	100	3.00/3.75	—	—	—	—	—	✓	No
South Dakota	25	11,843	930	—	2.00	—	—	—	✓	—	✓	No
Tennessee	21	146,000	2,000	—	3.00	—	—	—	—	—	—	—
Texas	44	81,681	1,185	2,146	1.00/1.75	—	—	—	✓	—	✓	No
Utah	31	420	574	583	1.00	—	—	—	—	—	✓	Yes
Vermont	30	129,500	—	2,238	3.50/5.50	—	—	—	✓	—	✓	No
Virginia	14	21,989	—	—	3.00+tax	—	—	—	—	—	✓	No
Washington	175	76,138	4,481	4,481	1.75/2.25	—	—	—	—	—	✓	No
West Virginia	19	—	197	429	2.00/4.00	—	—	—	✓	—	—	Yes
Wisconsin	45	478,529	599	4,506	2.25/2.75	—	—	—	—	—	✓	Yes
Wyoming	4	—	—	—	No Fee	—	—	—	—	—	—	—

*Alabama in process of developing State Parks.   **Maine did not reply to letter or questionnaire.

CANADA

Alberta	42	132,000	7	35	1.50/1.75	—	—	—	—	—	✓	Yes
British Columbia	109	5,467,000	—	5,700	2.00	—	—	—	—	—	✓	Yes
Manitoba	7	—	1,127	3,553	1.50/2.50	9/15.00	—	—	—	—	✓	Yes
New Brunswick	27	4,800	737	1,181	2.00/2.50	—	—	—	—	—	✓	No
Newfoundland	36	68,000	—	1,335	1.50	10.50	—	—	—	—	✓	Yes
Nova Scotia	16	3,520	—	1,150	2.50	—	—	—	—	—	✓	No
Northwest Territories	—	—	—	9	—	—	—	—	—	—	(car)	—
Ontario	96	10,000,000	1,600	18,400	3.50/4.00	—	—	5.00	—	—	✓	Yes
Prince Edward Island	19	779	205	905	3.00/4.00	—	—	—	—	—	✓	No
Quebec	14	—	1,352	4,481	3.00/4.00	—	—	—	—	—	✓	Yes
Saskatchewan	75	—	—	—	—	—	—	—	—	—	✓	—
Yukon	—	—	—	54	—	—	—	3.00	—	—	(car)	Yes